W9-BDR-920

Rights of the Accused

Other books in the Issues on Trial Series

Rights of the Accused

Michelle Lewis, Book Editor

GREENHAVEN PRESS

An imprint of Thomson Gale, a part of The Thomson Corporation

Detroit • New York • San Francisco • New Haven, Conn. • Waterville, Maine • London

THOMSON

*

™

GALE

Christine Nasso, *Publisher*
Elizabeth Des Chenes, *Managing Editor*

© 2007 Thomson Gale, a part of The Thomson Corporation.

Thomson and Star logo are trademarks and Gale and Greenhaven Press are registered trademarks used herein under license.

For more information, contact:
Greenhaven Press
27500 Drake Rd.
Farmington Hills, MI 48331-3535
Or you can visit our Internet site at http://www.gale.com

ALL RIGHTS RESERVED
No part of this work covered by the copyright hereon may be reproduced or used in any form or by any means—graphic, electronic, or mechanical, including photocopying, record-ing, taping, Web distribution, or information storage retrieval systems—without the written permission of the publisher.

Articles in Greenhaven Press anthologies are often edited for length to meet page require-ments. In addition, original titles of these works are changed to clearly present the main thesis and to explicitly indicate the author's opinion. Every effort is made to ensure that Greenhaven Press accurately reflects the original intent of the authors. Every effort has been made to trace the owners of copyrighted material.

Cover photograph reproduced by permission of Reuters/Corbis.

LIBRARY OF CONGRESS CATALOGING-IN-PUBLICATION DATA

Rights of the Accused / Michelle Lewis, book editor.
    p. cm. -- (Issues on trial)
  Includes bibliographical references and index.
  ISBN-13: 978-0-7377-2795-1 (hardcover)
  ISBN-10: 0-7377-2795-0 (hardcover)
  1. Criminal procedure--United States. 2. Due process of law--United States.
  I. Lewis, Michelle.
  KF9618.R55 2007
  345.73'056--dc22
                                                          2006038192

Printed in the United States of America
10 9 8 7 6 5 4 3 2 1

Contents

Chapter 1: The Presumption of Innocence

In *Coffin v. United States*, the Supreme Court rules that a defendant's constitutional rights are violated if the jury is not instructed to consider the defendant innocent unless proven guilty beyond a reasonable doubt.

A year after the 1895 *Coffin* decision, a well-known attorney discusses the meaning of the presumption of innocence standard and asserts that the reasoning behind the decision—that by not being instructed to presume the defendant's innocence, the jury was deprived of evidence—is unsound.

A professor specializing in the history of the law expands on the origins of the presumption of innocence maxim, relating the story of Irish attorney Leonard MacNally, the cited source of the phrase "innocent until proven guilty" in *Coffin*.

Chapter 2: The Right to Counsel

Chapter 3: The Right to a Trial by Jury

Chapter 4: The Right to Confront One's Accusers

Foreword

The U.S. courts have long served as a battleground for the most highly charged and contentious issues of the time. Divisive matters are often brought into the legal system by activists who feel strongly for their cause and demand an official resolution. Indeed, subjects that give rise to intense emotions or involve closely held religious or moral beliefs lay at the heart of the most polemical court rulings in history. One such case was *Brown v. Board of Education* (1954), which ended racial segregation in schools. Prior to *Brown*, the courts had held that blacks could be forced to use separate facilities as long as these facilities were equal to that of whites.

For years many groups had opposed segregation based on religious, moral, and legal grounds. Educators produced heartfelt testimony that segregated schooling greatly disadvantaged black children. They noted that in comparison to whites, blacks received a substandard education in deplorable conditions. Religious leaders such as Martin Luther King Jr. preached that the harsh treatment of blacks was immoral and unjust. Many involved in civil rights law, such as Thurgood Marshall, called for equal protection of all people under the law, as their study of the Constitution had indicated that segregation was illegal and un-American. Whatever their motivation for ending the practice, and despite the threats they received from segregationists, these ardent activists remained unwavering in their cause.

Those fighting against the integration of schools were mainly white southerners who did not believe that whites and blacks should intermingle. Blacks were subordinate to whites, they maintained, and society had to resist any attempt to break down strict color lines. Some white southerners charged that segregated schooling was *not* hindering blacks' education. For example, Virginia attorney general J. Lindsay Almond asserted, "With the help and the sympathy and the love and respect of the white people of the South, the colored man has risen under that educational process to a place of eminence and respect throughout the nation. It has served him well." So when the Supreme Court ruled against the segregationists in *Brown*, the South responded with vociferous cries of protest. Even government leaders criticized the decision. The governor of Arkansas, Orval Faubus, stated that he would not "be a party to any attempt to force acceptance of change to which the people are so overwhelmingly opposed." Indeed, resistance to integration was so great that when black students arrived at the formerly all-white Central High School in Arkansas, federal troops had to be dispatched to quell a threatening mob of protesters.

Nevertheless, the *Brown* decision was enforced and the South integrated its schools. In this instance, the Court, while not settling the issue to everyone's satisfaction, functioned as an instrument of progress by forcing a major social change. Historian David Halberstam observes that the *Brown* ruling "deprived segregationist practices of their moral legitimacy. . . . It was therefore perhaps the single most important moment of the decade, the moment that separated the old order from the new and helped create the tumultuous era just arriving." Considered one of the most important victories for civil rights, *Brown* paved the way for challenges to racial segregation in many areas, including on public buses and in restaurants.

In examining *Brown*, it becomes apparent that the courts play an influential role—and face an arduous challenge—in shaping the debate over emotionally charged social issues. Judges must balance competing interests, keeping in mind the high stakes and intense emotions on both sides. As exemplified by *Brown*, judicial decisions often upset the status quo and initiate significant changes in society. Greenhaven Press's Issues on Trial series captures the controversy surrounding influential court rulings and explores the social ramifications of such decisions from varying perspectives. Each anthology highlights one social issue—such as the death penalty, students' rights, or wartime civil liberties. Each volume then focuses on key historical and contemporary court cases that helped mold the issue as we know it today. The books include a compendium of primary sources—court rulings, dissents, and immediate reactions to the rulings—as well as secondary sources from experts in the field, people involved in the cases, legal analysts, and other commentators opining on the implications and legacy of the chosen cases. An annotated table of contents, an in-depth introduction, and prefaces that overview each case all provide context as readers delve into the topic at hand. To help students fully probe the subject, each volume contains book and periodical bibliographies, a comprehensive index, and a list of organizations to contact. With these features, the Issues on Trial series offers a well-rounded perspective on the courts' role in framing society's thorniest, most impassioned debates.

Introduction

> *"A society should not be judged on how it treats its outstanding citizens but by how it treats its criminals."*
>
> —*Fyodor Dostoyevsky*

The great Russian novelist Dostoyevsky, best known for his literary probe of a tormented murderer's psyche, *Crime and Punishment* (1866), makes an important point about the value of the rights of the accused to society. Like Dostoyevsky, many contemporary Western sociologists argue that the true beliefs of a society are reflected in the rights it grants members accused of a crime, no matter what the charge. Furthermore, they contend, the specific rights extended to the accused also reflect the problems of society and the judicial attempts to correct these problems.

This is certainly true for the four rights discussed in this book: the right to be presumed innocent until proven guilty, the right to counsel even if the accused cannot afford to pay for it, the right to a trial by jury, and the right to face one's accusers. Each of these rights has evolved over centuries of law codes; each is currently considered fundamental to a sound legal system and essential to achieving justice for the accused. The interpretation, application, and protection of these rights, even in the context of horrific acts, is to many the ultimate measure of American society.

Common-Law Origins

The presumption of innocence is the only one of the four rights that is not derived from an interpretation of the U.S. Constitution. Instead, this right is part of the common law; that is, an ancient idea refined through centuries of judicial decisions rather than drafted in writing as "black letter law"; that is, a law that has been drafted with specific wording and is not open to interpretation.

Although the presumption of innocence (and its companion principle, reasonable doubt) entered the American system in a case about white-collar crime (*Coffin v. United States*, 1895), the idea emerged in the English legal system in the mid-1700s, during trials in Ireland of men accused of treason. Before this time, to return a guilty verdict a jury had to be *convinced* of a defendant's guilt after hearing the prosecution's case. From this point on, the standard was less strict; to return a guilty verdict a jury only had to believe the defendant was guilty *beyond a reasonable doubt.*

Lowering that standard of proof has led some critics to charge that the burden of proof has shifted from the prosecution to the defense, weakening the presumption of innocence, because jurors are more likely to vote guilty if, for example, they have a gut feeling the defendant is innocent but cannot give a reason for their doubt. Upholding basic legal maxims in such cases, above all the need for evidence to overcome an initial presumption of innocence of the accused, is an important step in ensuring justice is served and the accused is treated fairly.

The right to legal counsel during trial is guaranteed in federal courts by the Sixth Amendment to the Constitution; however, in the early 1960s the Supreme Court was asked to determine if this right extended to state courts as well. This is a very important determination for the rights of those accused of a crime, as a large portion of criminal prosecutions occur under state law and therefore are tried in state courts. Before this time, states had had set penalty thresholds—for example, the case must warrant the death penalty—which had to be crossed before they committed tax dollars to provide counsel for those who were indigent and therefore lacked the money to pay a lawyer.

Thus, in *Gideon v. Wainwright*, the social issues centrally tied to the case were poverty and the use of public funds. The Court had to decide whether providing no-cost counsel to the poor was a fundamental right, and therefore to refuse to provide free legal counsel was unconstitutional. By affirming the right to counsel to be paid by tax dollars in the *Gideon* case, the Court took strides toward the goal of providing equal justice to all accused of a crime no matter how much money he or she had. Although American society is still struggling with the practical application of this principle, this is a further example of a society's consideration of the value and equality of all of its members.

The Sixth Amendment of the Constitution also provides the right to a jury trial in federal cases. As with the right to counsel, in the late 1960s the Supreme Court had to decide whether this right applied to cases within the state court system. Also similar to the right to counsel, states had set penalty thresholds for the right to a jury trial. Since the time of the founding of the American colonies, juries have been seen as a means to balance governmental power, such as the power of judges, with the voice of the people. So under *Duncan v. Louisiana*, the Court had to determine whether an accused should be able to choose being tried by his or her peers, rather than by a government official such as a judge.

This case involved further social issues, those of racism and desegregation. Louisiana had a long history of resisting desegregation, and the defendant was accused of a crime related to defending his black cousins who had been newly enrolled in what had been an all-white school. Once again, the Supreme Court was in a position of attempting to remedy social ills through judicial action. When the Supreme Court supported the defendant's right to a jury trial—including a black defendant accused of a crime within a system controlled by the white majority—its decision supported American society's egalitarian principles and recognized the problems of racism.

The Sixth Amendment to the Constitution also provi the right of those accused of a crime to face their accusers. This right is also called the right of confrontation. This right was created to increase the openness of the trial and to guarantee that the accused had a so-called adversarial trial; that is, the accused had the right to cross-examine or ask questions of witnesses that are designed to reveal the weaknesses of the accuser's testimony. This right was a reaction to one-sided court systems that did not follow adversarial procedures, such as the notorious Court of the Star Chamber, an English court that sat between 1487 and 1641. Because the sessions were held in secret and all evidence was in writing, with no juries, witnesses, or appeals, the power wielded by the Star Chamber was easy to abuse and such abuse became the usual course of business.

Although certainly not on a par with the abuses of the Star Chamber, the courts within the United States had weakened this right by interpreting it as less than absolute. In 1980, for example, the Supreme Court held that if a witness's testimony was sufficiently "reliable" it could be entered into evidence even if the witness was unavailable to appear in court. It was this less-than-absolute interpretation of the right to confrontation that was questioned in the 2004 case of *Crawford v. Washington*.

Although less connected to social issues than were the first three rights discussed above, this case does have social ramifications. It is an example of a conflict between two very differing views of how the Constitution should be interpreted and how rights of those accused of a crime should be protected. In *Crawford*, the Court decided that the less-than-absolute reading of the right to confrontation should be overturned, and the procedure should be brought closer to the literal right provided in the Sixth Amendment. This is a politically conservative approach to protecting the rights of the accused and is in contrast to the more broad, liberal interpretations of the

Constitution made by the Court in the 1960s. It remains, however, that the rights of those accused are protected by this decision, an admirable goal for a society seeking justice for all.

By providing particular rights during trial to those accused of a crime, the American judicial system and society can be positively judged by Dostoyevsky's standard. The presumption of innocence, the right to counsel by the indigent, the right to a jury trial, and the right to confront his or her accusers all work to forward the goal of equal justice under the law. *Issues on Trial: Rights of the Accused* examines four key cases in the protection of the rights of the accused and the interaction between these judicial decisions and the related social issues addressed by the judicial action.

4101430

The Presumption of Innocence

Chapter Preface

Case Overview: The case of *Coffin v. United States* (1895) focused on whether four Indianapolis bankers convicted of using their bank's funds as their own should receive a new trial because the judge refused to instruct the jurors that the defendants were to be considered innocent until proven guilty. He did instruct the jury that the defendants had to be found guilty beyond a reasonable doubt, and, seemingly equating the two standards, refused the second instruction as to a presumption of innocence as unnecessary. F.A. Coffin, one of the convicted bankers, and his codefendants sought a new trial on the grounds that the two instructions were different and both were required for the jury to give proper consideration to the case. These circumstances set the stage for the Supreme Court to define the concept of "presumption of innocence."

Justice Edward D. White wrote the unanimous opinion that awarded the bankers a new trial. In a famous commentary on the decision, White stated that the right to be innocent until proven guilty was self-evident and basic, and enforcing this rule was at the "foundation of the administration of our criminal law." He supported this statement with a discussion of Roman law and well-respected American and European legal writers such as Simon Greenleaf, Sir John Fortescue, Leonard McNally, Lord Matthew Hale, and Sir William Blackstone. He also discussed relevant well-known English and American cases that could be considered precedents for the Court's decision.

Having established the solid position of this idea in the Anglo-American legal tradition, White goes on to examine whether the presumption of innocence and the standard of guilt beyond a reasonable doubt were one and the same. If so, then the lack of the instruction about the presumption would not require a new trial, since the reasonable doubt standard was sufficiently covered by the trial judge; however, after reviewing the writings on the subject, the Court's opinion stated that the two are related but not the same. In the Court's view, the presumption of innocence is evidence in favor of the accused and reasonable doubt is a possible result of considering that evidence. Thus, a defendant could expect instructions as to both standards, and omission of these instructions could form the basis for a new trial.

White concluded that this protection was absolutely necessary because of "the inevitable tendency to obscure the results of a truth [that is, the presence of reasonable doubt] when the truth itself [the presumption of innocence] is forgotten or ignored." Based on this finding, the Supreme Court found that the lack of an instruction on the presumption of innocence required a new trial for the four accused bankers. Thus, it was through the *Coffin* decision that the maxim that a person accused of a crime is innocent until proven guilty formally entered American law.

Although the basic holding of *Coffin v. United States* was not challenged—the principle had been present in the law for a long time—particular aspects of the case have generated controversy, both at the time of the decision and since. For example, John Wigmore, a well-known attorney of the day, criticized the conclusion that the presumption of innocence was evidence in favor of the accused. Wigmore argued rather that the presumption set a high standard for the factual evidence to be convincing enough to convict the accused. He rejected the argument that the presumption had the strength of evidence, however. This idea is still being debated; as University of Arkansas law professor Steve Sheppard asserts, reasonable doubt has become so difficult for jurors to find that many juries are no longer effectively presuming innocence, making it much easier to convict someone accused of a crime.

A further recent issue with this principle is its application to date rape cases, where supporters of the accused have asserted that the plaintiff (the woman claiming she was raped) must be disbelieved in order to preserve the presumption of innocence. Law professor Sherry Colb dismisses this position, stating that the presumption does not affect consideration of the evidence, and only comes into play when the jurors determine that a reasonable doubt exists *after* consideration of the evidence. It is then that they must bring back a "not guilty" verdict based on the presumption. Thus, despite its long presence in jurisprudence, the exact application of the presumption of innocence, as established by *Coffin*, continues to be controversial to this day.

> "The principle that there is a presumption of innocence in favor of the accused is the undoubted law, axiomatic and elementary."

The Court's Majority Opinion: Criminal Defendants Are Considered Innocent Until Proven Guilty

Edward Douglass White

In 1894 four Indianapolis bankers—Theodore P. Haughey, F.A. Coffin, Percival B. Coffin, and A.S. Reed—were accused of embezzlement; that is, using the bank's funds for their own personal use and various other violations of laws governing banking conduct. During their trial, the judge refused to instruct the jury that the accused were innocent until proven guilty. Instead, he provided a variety of instructions about the need for finding guilt beyond a reasonable doubt, but fell short of telling the jurors to presume the bankers' innocence until their guilt was proven. The four were convicted but appealed the case to the Supreme Court. On March 4, 1895, Justice Edward Douglass White issued the Court's unanimous decision overturning the conviction because insufficient weight, or instruction, was given to the presumption of innocence, found to be a fundamental right of anyone accused of a crime in the American legal system. White's famous commentary is the following viewpoint. White served on the Supreme Court from 1894 until his death in 1921, serving as chief justice his last ten years on the bench.

Edward Douglass White, *Coffin v. United States*, 156 US 432 (1895).

The fact, then, is that, while the court refused to instruct as to the presumption of innocence, it instructed fully on the subject of reasonable doubt.

The principle that there is a presumption of innocence in favor of the accused is the undoubted law, axiomatic and elementary, and its enforcement lies at the foundation of the administration of our criminal law. . . .

[Simon] Greenleaf [in his book, *On Evidence*] traces this presumption to Deuteronomy, and quotes [Josef] Mascardius's De Probationibus to show that it was substantially embodied in the laws of Sparta and Athens. Whether Greenleaf is correct or not in this view, there can be no question that the Roman law was pervaded with the results of this maxim of criminal administration. . . .

Ammianus Marcellinus relates an anecdote of the Emperor Julian which illustrates the enforcement of this principle in the Roman law. Numerius, the governor of Narbonensis, was on trial before the emperor, and, contrary to the usage in criminal cases, the trial was public. Numerius contented himself with denying his guilt, and there was not sufficient proof against him. His adversary, Delphidius, 'a passionate man,' seeing that the failure of the accusation was inevitable, could not restrain himself, and exclaimed, 'Oh, illustrious Caesar! if it is sufficient to deny, what hereafter will become of the guilty?' to which Julian replied, 'If it suffices to accuse, what will become of the innocent?' (Rerum Gestarum, lib. 18, c. 1). The rule thus found in the Roman law was, along with many other fundamental and human maxims of that system, preserved for mankind by the canon law. . . . Exactly when this presumption was, in precise words, stated to be a part of the common law, is involved in doubt. The writer of an able article in the *American Review* (January, 1851), tracing the genesis of the principle, says that no express mention of the presumption of innocence can be found in the books of the common law earlier than the date of [Leonard] M[a]cNally's *Evidence* (1802). Whether this statement is correct is a matter of no moment, for there can be no doubt that, if the principle had not found formal expression in the common-law writers at an earlier date, yet the practice which flowed from it has existed in the common law from the earliest time.

[Sir John] Fortescue says [in his treatise on the laws of England]: 'Who, then, in England, can be put to death unjustly for any crime? since he is allowed so many pleas and privileges in favor of life. None but his neighbors, men of honest and good repute, against whom he can have no probable cause of exception, can find the person accused guilty. Indeed, one would much rather that twenty guilty persons should escape punishment of death than that one innocent person should be condemned and suffer capitally.'

Lord [Matthew] Hale (1678) says [in his book *Pleas of the Crown*]: 'In some cases presumptive evidence goes far to prove a person guilty, though there be no express proof of the fact to be committed by him; but then it must be very warily pressed, for it is better five guilty persons should escape unpunished than one innocent person should die.' He further observes: 'And thus the reasons stand on both sides; and, though these seem to be stronger than the former, yet in a case of this moment it is safest to hold that in practice, which hath least doubt and danger—[to quote Immanuel Kant]: 'Quod dubitas, ne feceris.' [What you doubt, you should not do.]

[William] Blackstone (1753–1765) maintains [in his *Commentaries*] that 'the law holds that it is better that ten guilty persons escape than that one innocent suffer.'

How fully the presumption of innocence had been evolved as a principle and applied at common law is shown in McKinley's Case (1817) where Lord [Adam] Gillies says: 'It is impossible to look at it [a treasonable oath which it was alleged that McKinley had taken] without suspecting, and thinking it probable, it imports an obligation to commit a capital crime. That has been and is my impression. But the presumption in favor of innocence is not to be redargued by mere suspicion. I am sorry to see, in this information, that the public prosecutor treats this too lightly. He seems to think that the law entertains no such presumption of innocence. I cannot listen to this. I conceive that this presumption is to be found in every code of law which has reason and religion and humanity for a foundation, it is a maxim which ought to be inscribed in indelible characters in the heart of every judge and juryman, and I was happy to hear from Lord Hermand he is inclined to give full effect to it. To overturn this, there must be legal evidence of guilt, carrying home a decree of conviction short only of absolute certainty.'

It is well settled that there is no error in refusing to give a correct charge precisely as requested, provided the instruction actually given fairly covers and includes the instruction asked. The contention here is that, inasmuch as the charge given by the court on the subject of reasonable doubt substantially embodied the statement of the presumption of innocence, therefore the court was justified in refusing, in terms, to mention the latter. This presents the question whether the charge that there cannot be a conviction unless the proof shows guilt beyond a reasonable doubt so entirely embodies the statement of presumption of innocence as to justify the court in refusing, when requested, to inform the jury concerning the latter. The authorities upon this question are few and unsatisfactory. . . .

It may be that the paucity of authority upon this subject results from the fact that the presumption of innocence is so elementary that instances of denial to charge it upon request have rarely occurred. Such is the view expressed in a careful article in the *Criminal Law Magazine* for January, 1889 (volume 11, p. 3): 'The practice of stating this principle to juries is so nearly universal that very few cases are found where error has been assigned upon the failure or refusal of the judge so to do.' But, whatever be the cause, authorities directly apposite are few and conflicting, and hence furnish no decisive solution of the question, which is further embarrassed by the fact that in some few cases the presumption of innocence and the doctrine of reasonable doubt are seemingly treated as synonymous. . . . In these cases, however, it does not appear that any direct question was made as to whether the presumption of innocence and reasonable doubt were legally equivalent; the language used simply implying that one was practically the same as the other, both having been stated to the jury.

Some of the text-books, also, in the same loose way, imply the identity of the two. [Sir James Fitzjames] Stephen, in his *History of the Criminal Law*, tells us that 'the presumption of innocence is otherwise stated by saying the prisoner is entitled to the benefit of every reasonable doubt.' So, although [William] Best, in his work on Presumptions, has fully stated the presumption of innocence, yet, in a note to Chamberlayne's edition of that author's work on Evidence. It is asserted that no such presumption obtains, and that 'apparently all that is meant by the statement thereof, as a principle of law, is this: If a man be accused of crime, he must be proved guilty beyond reasonable doubt.'

This confusion makes it necessary to consider the distinction between the presumption of innocence and reasonable doubt as if it were an original question. In order to determine whether the two are the equivalents of each other, we must first ascertain, with accuracy, in what each consists. Now, the presumption of innocence is a conclusion drawn by the law in favor of the citizen, by virtue whereof, when brought to trial upon a criminal charge, he must be acquitted, unless he is proven to be guilty. In other words, this presumption is an instrument of proof created by the law in favor of one accused, whereby his innocence is established until sufficient evidence is introduced to overcome the proof which the law has created. This presumption, on the one hand, supplemented by any other evidence he may adduce, and the evidence against him, on the other, constitute the elements from which the legal [decision is] drawn.

Greenleaf [in *On Evidence*] thus states the doctrine: 'As men do not generally violate the Penal Code, the law presumes every man innocent; but some men do transgress it, and therefore evidence is received to repel this presumption. This legal presumption of innocence is to be regarded by the jury, in every case, as matter of evidence, to the benefit of which the party is entitled.'

[William] Wills on Circumstantial Evidence says: 'In the investigation and estimate of criminatory evidence, there is an antecedent, prima facie presumption in favor of the innocence of the party accused, grounded in reason and justice not less than in humanity, and recognized in the judicial practice of all civilized nations, which presumption must prevail until it be destroyed by such an overpowering amount of legal evidence of guilt as is calculated to produce the opposite belief.' Best on Presumptions declares the presumption of innocence to be a 'presumptio juris'[presumption of law]. The same view is taken in the article in the *Criminal Law Magazine* for January, 1888, to which we have already referred. It says: 'This presumption is in the nature of evidence in his [i.e., the accused's] favor, and a knowledge of it should be communicated to the jury. Accordingly, it is the duty of the judge, in all jurisdictions, when requested, and in some when not requested, to explain it to the jury in his charge. The usual formula in which this doctrine is expressed is that every man is presumed to be innocent until his guilt is proved beyond a reasonable doubt. The accused is entitled, if he so requests it, . . . to have this rule of law expounded to the jury in this or in some equivalent form of expression.'

The fact that the presumption of innocence is recognized as a presumption of law . . . demonstrates that it is evidence in favor of the accused. For, in all systems of law, legal presumptions are treated as evidence giving rise to resulting proof, to the full extent of their legal efficacy.

Concluding, then, that the presumption of innocence is evidence in favor of the accused, introduced by the law in his behalf, let us consider what is 'reasonable doubt.' It is, of necessity, the condition of mind produced by the proof resulting from the evidence in the cause. It is the result of the proof, not the proof itself, whereas the presumption of innocence is one of the instruments of proof, going to bring about the proof from which reasonable doubt arises; thus one is a cause, the other an effect. To say that the one is the equivalent of the other is therefore to say that legal evidence can be excluded from the jury, and that such exclusion may be cured by instructing them correctly in regard to the method by which they are required to reach their conclusion upon the proof actually before them; in other words, that the exclusion of an important element of proof can be justified by correctly instructing as to the proof admitted. The evolution of the principle of the presumption of innocence, and its resultant, the doctrine of reasonable doubt, make more apparent the correctness of these views, and indicate the necessity of enforcing the one in order that the other may continue to exist. While Rome and the Mediaevalists taught that, wherever doubt existed in a criminal case, acquittal must follow, the expounders of the common law, in their devotion to human liberty and individual rights, traced this doctrine of doubt to its true origin—the presumption of innocence—and rested it upon this enduring basis. The inevitable tendency to obscure the results of a truth, when the truth itself is forgotten or ignored, admonishes that the protection of so vital and fundamental a principle as the presumption of innocence be not denied, when requested, to any one accused of crime. The importance of the distinction between the two is peculiarly emphasized here, for, after having declined to instruct the jury as to the presumption of innocence, the court said: 'If, after weighing all the proofs, and looking only to the proofs, you impartially and honestly entertain the belief,' etc. Whether thus confining them to 'the proofs,' and only to the proofs, would have been error, if the jury had been instructed that the presumption of innocence was a part of the legal proof, need not be considered, since it is clear that the failure to instruct them in regard to it excluded from their minds a portion of the proof created by law, and which they were bound to consider. 'The proofs, and the proofs only,' confined them to those matters which were admitted to their consideration by the court; and, among these elements of proof, the court expressly refused to include the presumption of innocence, to which the accused was entitled, and the benefit whereof both the court and the jury were bound to extend him. . . .

Judgment reversed and case remanded, with directions to grant a new trial.

> *"The effect of the presumption of inno-*
> *cence, so far from being that of fur-*
> *nishing to the jury evidence ... is*
> *rather the contrary."*

The Presumption of Innocence Is Not Evidence of Innocence

John H. Wigmore

The Coffin *decision had a significant impact on legal thinking in the late nineteenth century. The author of the following article, John H. Wigmore, a noted attorney of the day, discusses what was believed to be the function of the presumption of innocence in criminal cases and supports the Supreme Court's upholding of this function in* Coffin. *He goes on to criticize the decision, however, for the conclusion that the presumption of innocence was evidence, and thus the jury was deprived of evidence by not receiving the instruction from the judge about the presumption of the defendants' innocence. Instead, Wigmore declares that it is only a legal conclusion, at most a mere substitute for evidence of innocence at the beginning of the trial, and sets the standard for how much evidence to the contrary must be presented to overcome the presumption and properly find the defendant guilty.*

Always, of course, there was operating in favor of the accused the sound maxim of general jurisprudence that the plaintiff or, rather, the party who seeks to move the court,

John H. Wigmore, "The Presumption of Innocence in Criminal Cases," reprinted in James Bradley Thayer, *A Preliminary Treatise on Evidence at the Common Law*. Boston: Little, Brown, 1898, pp. 551–76.

must make out a reason for his request. . . . That is a maxim of policy and practical sense; it is not founded on any notion that defendants generally are free from blame. It is a maxim or principle that saves the defendant by the mere inertia of the court, if the plaintiff does not make out his case. This maxim, in this bare form, and without the familiar additional clause as to the greater force of persuasion in criminal cases, always operated for the accused. It is probably true that in the form last given it has sometimes been mistranslated, and given a special application to criminal cases. . . .

In this country and in recent times, much emphasis in criminal cases has been put on the presumption of innocence. Always and everywhere great emphasis was placed on the rule that in criminal cases there can be no conviction unless guilt is established with very great clearness—as we say nowadays, beyond reasonable doubt. In civil cases it is enough if the mere balance of probability is with the plaintiff, but in criminal cases there must be a clear, heavy, emphatic preponderance.

The Meaning of the Presumption

Now, what does the presumption of innocence mean? Does it mean anything more than a particular application of that general rule of sense and convenience, running through all the law, that men in general are taken, . . . in the absence of evidence to the contrary, to be good, honest, free from blame, presumed to do their duty in every situation in life; so that no one need go forward, whether in pleading or proof, to show as regards himself or another, that the fact is so, but every one shall have it presumed in his favor? If it does, what is its meaning? . . .

The effect of the presumption of innocence, so far from being that of furnishing to the jury evidence—*i.e.*, probative matter, the basis of an inference—is rather the contrary. It takes possession of this fact, innocence as not now needing evidence, as already established *prima facie* [at first view], and says: "Take that for granted. Let him who denies it, go forward with his evidence." In criminal cases if the jury were not thus called off from the field of natural inference, if they were allowed to range there wherever mere reason and human experience would carry them, the whole purpose of the presumption of innocence would be balked. For of the men who are actually brought up for trial, probably the large majority are guilty. In inquiring lately of a prosecuting officer in Massachusetts for the statistics about this, he replied that out of every one hundred persons indicted for crime in his jurisdiction, twenty were tried and acquitted, twenty pleaded guilty, and sixty were tried and convicted. Now the presumption of innocence forbids the consideration of such probabilities as are here suggested and says simply this: "It is the right of this man to be convicted upon legal evidence applicable specifically to him. Start then with the assumption that he is innocent, and adhere to it till he is proved guilty. He is indeed under grave suspicion, and it is your duty to test and fairly to weigh all the evidence against him as well as for him. But he is not to suffer in your minds from these suspicions or this necessity of holding him confined and trying him; he is to be affected by nothing but such evidence as the law allows you to act upon. For the purposes of this trial you must take him to be an innocent man, unless and until the government establishes his guilt." . . .

Presumption and Evidence Are Separate

As to the real nature of the rule about a presumption of innocence, an important intimation is contained in Chief Justice Shaw's[1] phrase that, "All the presumptions of law *independent of evidence* are in favor of innocence." That appears to be accurate and exact. The presumption is "independent of evidence," being the same in all cases; and in all operating indis-

1. Lemuel Shaw was the chief justice of the Massachusetts Supreme Court from 1830 to 1860. He was highly influential at not only the state but also the federal level.

criminately, in the same way, and with equal force. On what is it founded? On the fact that men in general do not commit crime? On what is the presumption of sanity founded? On the fact that men in general are sane? Perhaps so, as a legislative reason, so to speak, or one of the reasons. But the rule itself is a different thing from the grounds of it, and when we speak of the presumption of innocence or of sanity we are talking of a legal rule of presumption, a legal position, and not of the facts which are the basis of it. . . .

Comparing *Coffin*

Let me return now to the case of *Coffin v. U.S.* It will be necessary to consider it in some detail. It came up from the Circuit Court of the United States for Indiana, and was a proceeding against officials of a national bank who were convicted below [i.e., in a lower court] of wilfully misapplying funds of the bank, and of other related offences. A great number of exceptions were taken to the charge given by the court to the jury. All but two of these were overruled. The principal exception was against the refusal of the judge to charge as he was requested on the subject of the presumption of innocence. He had been asked to charge that, "the law presumes that persons charged with crime are innocent until they are proved by competent evidence to be guilty. To the benefit of this presumption the defendants are all entitled, and this presumption stands as their sufficient protection unless it has been removed by evidence proving their guilt beyond a reasonable doubt." The judge refused to give this charge, but instructed the jury that they could not find the defendants guilty unless satisfied of their guilt beyond a reasonable doubt, and he said: "If you can reconcile the evidence with any reasonable hypothesis consistent with the defendant's innocence, it is your duty to do so. In that case find defendant not guilty. And if, after weighing all the proofs, and looking only to the proofs, you impartially and honestly entertain the belief that the defendant may be innocent of the offences charged against him, he is entitled to the benefit of that doubt, and you should acquit him." In various forms the judge went on to explain what "a reasonable doubt" is, and to make very clear the duty of the jury as to the weight of evidence which they were bound to require before they could find guilt.

The Supreme Court held that there was error in refusing the charge which was desired on the presumption of innocence; and, while recognizing that no particular form of words was necessary, in dealing with this presumption, they held that the error was not made good by anything found in the rest of the charge. The opinion of the [Supreme] Court was given by Mr. Justice White, and was not accompanied by any expression of dissent. . . .

Such was the decision, in *Coffin v. U. S.*, so far as relates to the point now under consideration, and such the general course of the exposition. It proceeds, in a word, on the ground that the lower court refused to recognize the presumption of innocence, and thus kept from the jury a piece of evidence in behalf of the accused to which he was entitled. The immediate result of the decision was that it helped to delay the punishment of persons well deserving it, as appeared when the case came back again after another trial, and when all of "very numerous grounds of error" urged by these defendants were overruled. . . .

That opinion, however, has had an effect outside of the particular case. Its somewhat wider range than common, of reference and allusion, has caused the imputing to it of an amount of learning and careful research to which, when scrutinized, it can lay no claim: and, to be quite just, it does not, in fact, lay claim to it. . . . Instead of settling anything outside of the particular controversy, it leaves matters worse off than before. Its work of mischief may be seen in the use of it in later cases. . . . The difficulty with the case is not with the actual decision—namely, that on the point in question a new trial should be granted; that could easily be agreed to, without any serious difference as to the principal matters. The trouble is with the exposition and the reasons.

Wigmore's Conclusions

What appears to be true may be stated thus:

1. A presumption operates to relieve the party in whose favor it works from going forward in argument or evidence.

2. It serves therefore the purposes of a *prima facie* case, and in that sense it is, temporarily, the substitute or equivalent for evidence.

3. It serves this purpose until the adversary has gone forward with his evidence. How much evidence shall be required from the adversary to meet the presumption, or, as it is variously expressed, to overcome it or destroy it, is determined by no fixed rule. It may be merely enough to make it reasonable to require the other side to answer; it may be enough to make out a full *prima facie* case, and it may be a great weight of evidence, excluding all reasonable doubt.

4. A mere presumption involves no rule as to the weight of evidence necessary to meet it. When a presumption is called a strong one, like the presumption of legitimacy, it means that it is accompanied by another rule relating to the weight of evidence to be brought in by him against whom it operates.

5. A presumption itself contributes no evidence, and has no probative quality. It is sometimes said that the presumption will tip the scale when the evidence is balanced. But, in truth, nothing tips the scale but evidence, and a presumption—being a legal rule or a legal conclusion—is not evidence. It may represent and spring from certain evidential facts; and these facts may be put in

the scale. But that is not putting in the presumption itself. A presumption may be called "an instrument of proof," in the sense that it determines from whom evidence shall come, and it may be called something "in the nature of evidence," for the same reason; or it may be called a substitute for evidence, and even "evidence"—in the sense that it counts at the outset, for evidence enough to make a *prima facie* case. But the moment these conceptions give way to the perfectly distinct notion of evidence proper—*i.e.*, probative matter, which may be a basis of inference, something capable of being weighed in the scales of reason and compared and estimated with other matter of the probative sort—so that we get to treating the presumption of innocence or any other presumption, as being evidence in this its true sense, then we have wandered into the region of shadows and phantoms.

| *"There are few maxims that have a greater resonance in Anglo-American, common law jurisprudence."*

The Concept of "Innocent Until Proven Guilty" Long Predates *Coffin*

Kenneth Pennington

Although the presumption that a criminal defendant is innocent until proven guilty may now seem like common sense, this idea developed over centuries from very early European judicial thought to its application in modern American courts. Ultimately, it became law in America with the Coffin *decision. In this excerpt Catholic University of America law professor Kenneth Pennington discusses the* Coffin *decision and Justice Edward D. White's reference to an Irish legal writer, Leonard MacNally, for the expression of this thought in English law. Pennington describes the views MacNally propounded while he was defending Irishmen accused of treason. He also briefly describes the work of Italian legal writer Cesare Beccaria, to whom MacNally attributes the presumption of innocence in his writing. Thus, this essay points out the international acceptance and the international roots of one of the most basic tenets in American jurisprudence, the maxim that the accused is innocent until proven guilty.*

Kenneth Pennington, "Innocent Until Proven Guilty: The Origins of a Legal Maxim," http://classes.maxwell.syr.edu/his381/InnocentuntilGuilty.htm. © 1999 Kenneth Pennington. Reproduced by permission of the author.

The maxim "Innocent until proven guilty" has had a good run in the twentieth century. The United Nations incorporated the principle in its Declaration of Human Rights in 1948 under article eleven, section one. The maxim also found a place in the European Convention for the Protection of Human Rights in 1953 (as article 6, section 2) and was incorporated into the United Nations International Covenant on Civil and Political Rights (as article 14, section 2) [ratified in 1976]. This was a satisfying development for Americans, because there are few maxims that have a greater resonance in Anglo-American common-law jurisprudence. The Anglo-American reverence for the maxim does pose an interesting conundrum: it cannot be found in the Magna Carta, the English Bill of Rights of 1689, the Declaration of Independence, or in the Constitution of the United States; and not, I might add, in the works of the great English jurists [Henry] Bracton, [Edward] Coke, and [William] Blackstone. Nevertheless, some scholars have claimed that the maxim has been firmly embedded in English jurisprudence since earliest times. . .

Entry into American Law

We can know exactly when the maxim formally entered American law: through a Supreme Court decision of 1895, *Coffin vs. U.S.* A lower court had refused to instruct the jury that "The law presumes that persons charged with crime are innocent until they are proven by competent evidence to be guilty." The appeal to the Supreme Court was based in part on the lower court's refusal.

Although the lower court rejected the maxim, the judge did instruct the jury that "Before you can find any one of the defendants guilty you must be satisfied of his guilt as charged in some of the counts of the indictment beyond a reasonable doubt." The lower court then instructed the jury at great length on the doctrine of reasonable doubt and its relationship to evidence. The Supreme Court saw its task as determining whether the lower court had violated the defendants' rights by not instructing the jury on presumption of innocence and whether reasonable doubt was essentially the same as presumption of innocence.

Justice Edward Douglass White wrote the majority opinion. For a legal historian, his analysis is a dazzling display of legal history—even if most of it is wrong. To prove the antiquity of "Innocent until proven guilty" White cited a story from the late antique Roman historian, Ammianus Marcellinus, and texts from Justinian's *Digest and Code*, Pope Gregory IX's *Decretales*, a decretal of Pope Innocent III, and Giuseppe Mascardi's *De probationibus*, all of these works, except for Ammianus, from the [European] continental law. None of the texts, unfortunately, contained the maxim. Not one of them was from English law.

When White turned to the Anglo-American tradition, he found the principle clearly articulated in a number of nineteenth-century treatises on evidence and criminal law. The jurists White cited were William Wills (*On Circumstantial Evidence*), Simon Greenleaf (*On the Law of Evidence*), and William Best (*On Presumptions*). Of these jurists, Best is the only one who explicitly states that it is a "maxim of law, that every person must be presumed innocent until proven guilty."

Crediting Irish Legalist Leonard MacNally

Justice White did try and trace the maxim in the English common law tradition but could only find one piece of evidence. He cited an anonymous author of an article in the *North American Review* of 1851 who stated that the maxim is first found in a treatise on evidence by an Irish jurist named Leonard MacNally. White concluded that even "if the principle had not yet found formal expression in the common law writers at an earlier date, yet the practice which flowed from it has existed in the common law from earliest time."

In *Coffin v. U.S.* Justice White ordained Leonard MacNally as the midwife of "Innocent until proven guilty"'s entrance into the American common law tradition. Who was he? The anonymous author of the *Dictionary of National Biography*'s [DNB] article on MacNally alleged that he was "no great lawyer" but an "astute and eloquent advocate." His dismissal of MacNally's legal skills does the Irish barrister a grave disservice. The DNB's author did not realize that MacNally's *The Rules of Evidence on Pleas of the Crown Illustrated from Printed and Manuscript Trials and Cases,* published in Dublin and London 1802, was immediately transported across the Atlantic and printed in Philadelphia 1804 and reprinted in 1811. One cannot read American treatises on evidence and presumption in the first half of the nineteenth century without stumbling over MacNally.

The Role of Treason

MacNally was particularly important for the development of rules governing evidence and procedure in criminal cases because he had represented a number of United Irishmen accused of treason. He quotes a large number of his own cases in his book. It is no fluke that treason led MacNally to consider the rules of evidence more carefully than previous writers. The cases that society has found most heinous have always been those in which the rules of fair and just procedure have come under attack.

The rules of procedure for cases of treason were still substantially different from the normal rules of criminal procedure in eighteenth-century Ireland. During MacNally's lifetime the same rules of due process enjoyed by English defendants were not extended to Irishmen defendants in treason trials. Although two statutes of King Edward VI and another of William III required two witnesses for any conviction of treason, this procedural nicety was not extended to Irishmen. MacNally emphasized the presumption of innocence for those accused of treason and justified applying the same rules of due process to them as to other defendants of criminal offences. His defense of Irish rights was fierce, and he argued vehemently for the rights of defendants, often using examples from cases in which he had participated. Although MacNally never quoted our maxim, he came very close to stating the principle when he discussed the two-witness rule for cases of treason by citing Cesare Beccaria.

> In Beccaria's judgment, one witness is not sufficient; for whilst the accused denies what the other affirms, truth remains suspended, and the right that every one has to be believed innocent turns the balance in his favour.

A century later Justice White may have used this passage from MacNally to plant the doctrine of presumption of innocence firmly in American jurisprudence. Let me note an important caveat here: White does not give a specific citation, and from the wording of his opinion, he may not have even looked at MacNally's book.

A "Traitor" Himself?

MacNally's story does, however, have a darker side. After his death in 1820 the English press revealed that MacNally had played the role of a double agent since at least 1794. While he was representing Irish revolutionaries as their defense attorney in court, he was betraying them to the government by passing on key information. He relayed all the details about the revolutionary activities that he received from his clients to the government prosecutors. From 1800 until his death he received 300 [pounds] a year [about $25,000 in present-day dollars] for his trouble. Of this side of MacNally, Justice White knew nothing.

One may ask, from where did MacNally get his principles? MacNally acknowledged Beccaria, and, indeed, Cesare did extoll presumption of innocence several times in his famous treatise, *Dei delitti e delle pene* (*On Crimes and Punishments*). He argued for always having two witnesses before one could be condemned for a criminal offence:

> More than one witness is needed, because, so long as one party affirms and the other denies, nothing is certain and the right triumphs that every man has to be believed innocent.

A few pages later, Beccaria repeated the same argument when, in the most passionate page of his tract, he assailed torture.

> Either the crime is certain or it is not; if it is certain, then no other punishment is called for than what is established by law and other torments are superfluous because the criminal's confession is superfluous; if it is not certain, then according to the law, you ought not torment an innocent because such is a man whose crimes have not been proven.

MacNally relied on Cesare Beccaria to justify presumption of innocence.

| "Federal and state judges have directly attacked the articulable doubt standard on the grounds that it reverses the presumption of innocence."

Changes to *Coffin*'s Standard of Reasonable Doubt Weaken the Presumption of Innocence

Steve Sheppard

The standard of proof for a criminal conviction—guilt beyond a reasonable doubt—and the presumption of innocence have long been connected in legal jurisprudence. In the following article, Steve Sheppard, a law professor at the University of Arkansas, argues that the understanding of what is reasonable, and therefore what constitutes "a reasonable doubt," has changed over time. Specifically, he asserts that the standard has evolved from an abstract philosophical relationship between man and the nature of judgment to a much more simplistic formula of whether or not a juror can articulate the reasons behind his doubts. By lowering the standard for reasonable doubt to such a simple formula, it seems that the accused is no longer presumed innocent until proven guilty. Instead, Sheppard claims, the accused is guilty until the defense has provided some hole or deficiency in the state's case that the juror can point to as a reason to acquit. Not only is the presumption of innocence lost, but Sheppard also states that this approach immorally infringes on the juror's independent judgment of the evidence.

Steve Sheppard, "The Metamorphoses of Reasonable Doubt: How Changes in the Burden of Proof Have Weakened the Presumption of Innocence," *Notre Dame Law Review*, vol. 78, May 2003, pp. 1237-42, 1244-45. © by Notre Dame Law Review, University of Notre Dame. Reprinted with permission.

From the very beginning, the reasonable-doubt instruction was intertwined with the presumption of innocence. The state held the burden of persuasion, who must prove or disprove guilt, and the burden of proof established whether the state had met its obligation, by setting how sufficiently the state had proved the defendant's guilt. These two separate obligations are merged in the claim that the government must prove the defendant's guilt beyond a reasonable doubt. Therefore, even though the two standards are usually subject to separate instructions, when the Supreme Court adopted the reasonable-doubt standard as an interpretation of due process, it also enshrined the standard of a presumption of innocence as a constitutional requirement. . . .

Federal and state judges have directly attacked the articulable doubt standard[1] on the grounds that it reverses the presumption of innocence. This concern is highlighted in cases in which a holdout juror is required to explain that juror's point of view, after which the holdout accepts the majority's view of the evidence.

The Significance of Reasonable-Doubt Instruction Has Changed

[Originally, the reasonable-doubt standard was supported by] careful divisions by the likes of [John] Locke[2] and [Simon] Greenleaf[3] [and] were built on an idea of reason as the nature of judgment. It was a complicated affair, in which there was considerable room for the reasonable but unexpressed and inexpressible.

During the nineteenth and twentieth centuries, however, the focus of something reasonable, particularly a reasonable thought, became increasingly simple, if not increasingly sim-

1. This standard for reasonable doubt requires jurors to be able to state the basis for their concerns. It is discussed further below.
2. A seventeenth-century English political philosopher.
3. A respected author of a treatise on evidence, he was a professor at Harvard Law School in the 1830s and 1840s.

plistic. First it became necessarily important. Then it became necessarily quantifiable. The love affair with reduction of the complex to the simple and the moral to the rational led to a linguistic drift that was rarely noticeable at any given time but profound in its ultimate effects.

Over time, the loss of our understanding of moral certainty and the increasing acceptance of articulability as a basis for reasonableness underscored a great shift in thinking about judgment by a juror. The courts have moved the jurors' goal from a vote for the state if the state can convince them of a fact to a vote for the state unless the defense can convince them of a certain type of doubt. This shift highlights two fundamental concerns regarding the role of the juror, and our beliefs about that role.

The Change May Fundamentally Alter the Presumption of Innocence

The shift appears to reverse the presumption of guilt. Although empirical research is necessary to determine whether this result occurs as easily as it seems, articulability instructions may work in the following way. A juror who would vote to convict may feel quite comfortable in the jury room in saying, "I think he's guilty," or at most, "The state has proved his guilt to me beyond a reasonable doubt." There is no apparent sense that such a juror is required to relate or even understand the state's case in detail.

A juror who would vote to acquit following an articulability instruction faces a different requirement. Because a reasonable doubt is one for which a reason must be given, this juror would seem to be obliged to say precisely what the doubt with the state's case is and why it is reasonable. A mere declaration that the juror is not convinced does not seem enough; it lacks the specificity suggested.

Of course, if the juror is not convinced, then according to the presumption of innocence, the juror is supposed to feel free to vote to acquit. This supposition may be false in the light of the tremendous imbalance in favor of the state suggested by an articulable doubt instruction. The defendant—in the face of the modern reasonable-doubt instruction—must convince the jury of his innocence. . . .

The burden to justify a reasonable doubt places an added barrier to the juror who would argue against the state, and it is a barrier that is both different in kind and degree from any obligation held by a juror who would vote with the state. This burden, created at the dawn of the reasonable-doubt instruction, although little appreciated for what it was, has simply grown more visible with the dumbing down of reasonable-doubt instructions over time. . . .

The Instruction Intrudes on Juror Discretion

A further consideration that arises from this examination is that it highlights the very nature of the instruction as a limitation on the discretion of the juror. The instruction represents an attempt by the experts of the legal system to impose a series of limits on how the jurors will use their discretion. They are not to act independently but only as the law would have them act in their role. This particular limit on discretion is one that might be fundamentally immoral. . . .

The juror has been given a task that demands only one power, the discretion to reach an independent judgment. A limitation on the forms of judgment the juror may apply to the evidence presented in the trial is a limit on discretion, on the powers necessary to perform that task. Looking at the sum of the moral notions that might apply in the state's obligations to the juror, there is no question that the limit of juror independence is an immoral burden placed by state officials on the citizen-juror.

The moral problem of limited juror independence is heightened once the lens of the burdens on the juror is widened to encompass not only the decision itself but also the legal and social responsibility for the decision. Simply put, the juror is blamed for the law's errors.

The successes and mistakes in investigation, arrest, and prosecution are placed before the jury. The jury alone must decide the facts of the case and the guilt of the accused. Once that decision is reached, the scrutiny that is made of it is very limited. A judge, whether in trial or on appeal, must set aside a jury verdict only if the judge believes the verdict is so outrageous that no reasonable jury could reach it. So long as the evidence presented in the case makes a decision a close call, a judge is unlikely to disturb a jury verdict. Thus, the harder the case, the more judicial reliance on the jury's decision there will likely be.

The jury is a scapegoat for the law. The juror immunizes the police, judge, and lawyers from mistakes prior to trial. Judges will not correct mistakes made by police or the lawyers or other judges unless the jury would likely have reached another decision if the mistake had not occurred. And, jurors immunize mistakes made after the trial. Judges need not much concern themselves that the condemned defendant is innocent, as that was a job for the jury. An actual error, the wrongful conviction of an innocent, is the fault of the jury. . . .

There Is a Need for Further Research

It is clear that the current standard of proof beyond a reasonable doubt has deep normative and descriptive frailties. There remains, however, an empirical gap of whether, in any one case, a jury is more likely to reach an historically accurate and morally justified verdict by one instruction or another. How much influence the instructions have in jury deliberations is difficult to measure, and how much of a difference one instruction might have over another must be a tremendously fact-intensive and context-sensitive endeavor. . . .

The holy grail of criminal law is to set its procedures so that all criminal defendants who have, in fact, committed crimes are punished for these crimes, but all those who are innocent but arrested are acquitted. Although there are those who believe that perfection in criminal law is dangerous to pursue, a standard of procedure in which this level of protection and inquisition would be achieved would be by that very fact justified; a truly more accurate criminal process would have both more convictions and fewer false convictions. Furthermore, all of the agents who act in accordance with such a marvelous standard would be acting with a sound basis that the retributive and social goals of the law are satisfied by their conduct.

> "In truth, every one of us is free, both
> factually and legally, to think whatever
> we wish about the guilt or innocence of
> a defendant."

The Presumption
of Innocence Applies to
Date Rape Cases

Sherry F. Colb

*Certain legal situations can complicate the application of the
principle that the accused is innocent until proven guilty. One
example of this is in the case of rape where the accused and the
accuser are acquainted, so-called date rape. Some analysts argue
that if the accused rapist is to be presumed innocent, then the
accuser must be presumed to be lying. This argument has been
used as justification for questioning the stories of accusers in date
rape cases. But in the following article, Rutgers School of Law–
Newark professor Sherry Colb explains why this is an improper
application of the legal concept. She states that the presumption
does not require the jurors to make advance decisions about the
evidence; rather, they are bound to consider with an open mind
all evidence as it is presented. Not until the final verdict decision
does the presumption actually comes into play, according to
Colb. At that time, after a fair and impartial consideration of all
the evidence, if guilt is not proven beyond a reasonable doubt
then the default decision is that the accused must be found inno-*

Sherry F. Colb, "Date Rape: Misconceptions about Presumption of Innocence," *CNN.com
Law Center*, October 28, 2003. Originally appeared on writ.findlaw.com. Reproduced by
permission of the author.

cent. Thus, the "guilty until proven innocent" maxim, if applied correctly, does not support prejudgment of any aspect of the evidence in a date rape case.

Misconceptions abound when it comes to the presumption of innocence. One of them may surface in the extremely controversial Kobe Bryant rape prosecution.[1] Some have suggested that the presumption of innocence, in a case like Bryant's, amounts to a presumption that the accuser is lying.

What Does the Presumption of Innocence Mean?

Many non-lawyers (and even some lawyers) mistakenly hold the following view of the presumption of innocence: that unless and until a defendant has been proved guilty beyond a reasonable doubt to the satisfaction of a jury, he remains actually innocent.

On this flawed (and even preposterous) understanding of the law, no one may permissibly believe that a defendant charged with a crime is guilty, if a jury has not already so concluded. In truth, every one of us is free, both factually and legally, to think whatever we wish about the guilt or innocence of a defendant, regardless of what a jury has said or will say on the matter.

The presumption of innocence is a requirement that applies only to the members of a jury in a criminal trial. Even as to them, moreover, it does not dictate jurors' thoughts. It simply obligates them to select "not guilty" as their verdict if the prosecution fails to produce sufficient evidence to persuade them of a defendant's guilt beyond a reasonable doubt.

Members of criminal juries that ultimately acquit may and often do conclude, based on the evidence, that the defendant

1. Kobe Bryant, a member of the Los Angeles Lakers professional basketball team, was accused of raping a nineteen-year-old woman in Colorado the evening of June 30, 2003. The case went as far as jury selection but was ultimately dismissed on September 7, 2004.

is actually guilty. That evidentiary reality is both unobjectionable and statistically inevitable, given the weighty burden of proof borne by the prosecution.

What the Presumption Requires of Rape Case Jurors

A related notion regarding the presumption of innocence is that it obligates jurors and potential jurors to believe at the outset that a rape complainant is probably lying when she accuses a defendant of date rape.

Though "date rape" is not a technical legal term, I use it here to distinguish rapes in which the victim and perpetrator are acquainted with each other prior to the crime, from "stranger rapes," in which the victim first encounters her attacker at the time of the assault. Because there is virtually no risk of mistaken identification in cases of date rape, a conclusion that the defendant did not rape the complainant almost always carries with it the implication that the accuser has leveled a false accusation against the defendant.

Consider why this implication is almost inescapable in date rape trials. In a stranger rape case, the accuser ordinarily has selected the defendant out of a lineup or mug book as the perpetrator. To believe that the defendant is innocent in such a case accordingly does not require anyone to think ill of the complaining witness. The defendant's supporters, on the contrary, may (and most often do) believe the victim's account of being raped but believe as well that she is mistaken about who committed the crime.

Making an honest mistake is no crime, and it is therefore possible to view the defendant as innocent without viewing the victim as anything other than a sincere person and an actual victim (albeit of another perpetrator) who deserves justice. If the presumption of innocence demanded skepticism about the prosecutor's case, then, such skepticism would not involve thinking any less of the complainant's character in stranger rape cases.

A Special Case for Date Rape?

Contrast this state of affairs with the date rape context. Here, the complaining witness and the defense typically agree that intercourse occurred between defendant and accuser. The main dispute is over whether the defendant acted with or without the accuser's consent. That is the case in the Kobe Bryant prosecution, for example.

Because the difference between rape and consensual sex is a memorable one for a victim, the defense is unlikely to propose that the complainant is simply mistaken in her recollection of what occurred between her and the defendant. The defense is far more apt to propose that any discrepancy between the defendant's and the complainant's versions of what occurred reflects false testimony on the part of the latter.

There is naturally no polite or sympathetic way to suggest that an accuser is making a false rape accusation. For that reason, a juror who interprets the presumption of innocence as requiring an attitude of skepticism and incredulity in the face of the prosecutor's evidence will necessarily adopt an unflattering and even hostile view of the complaining witness.

Some believe, in keeping with this reasoning, that it is incumbent upon jurors in date rape cases to approach the evidence with the assumption that the person who says she is a victim is actually a false accuser. If that were the law that applied to jurors, then no one could be blamed for regarding Kobe Bryant's accuser with suspicion and disbelief.

The Presumption Allows Jurors to Come to Their Own Conclusions

As it turns out, the presumption of innocence requires no such thing of jurors. It does not tell the jury to assume that prosecution witnesses are either mistaken or lying. Like members of the public at large, the judge does not instruct jurors in a criminal case on what to think. Jurors properly instructed on the law are consequently free to accept any given witness's story.

In determining whether to believe a witness, jurors can thus rely on the witness's demeanor, his ability to respond to questions on cross-examination, and the overall plausibility of his account of the events in question. They can also take into consideration any systematic (or particular) biases that a witness brings to the proceedings. For example, jurors may permissibly consider—in weighing Kobe Bryant's testimony—the fact that he has an incentive to say that he is innocent, regardless of the truth; his freedom and his successful career hang in the balance.

In other words, the presumption of innocence does not require jurors to be any more skeptical of the prosecutor's witnesses than they are of the defendant's. They should approach all of the evidence with an open mind and bring their insight to bear on processing the testimony and evidentiary exhibits that they consider.

The Presumption Comes into Play Only at the Verdict

The presumption of innocence governs only the jury's answer to the verdict question. The jury must find the defendant "not guilty" if a fair and impartial consideration of the evidence leads the jury to conclude that guilt has not been proved beyond a reasonable doubt. When the prosecution presents witnesses in a stranger rape case, the jury does not have to presume that the prosecution witnesses are mistaken. And when the prosecution offers testimony in a date rape case, the jury is likewise not required to presume that the accuser is lying.

The reflexive hostility that some of Kobe Bryant's defenders have shown toward his accuser therefore exhibits no fidelity to the presumption of innocence. It instead prejudges the case before the evidence has been presented.

Of course, members of the public are free to prejudge the case on the basis of their emotional investments and blink at reality as they wish. But the one thing that a jury must never do is decide in advance to presume to reject testimony and evidence that it has not yet heard.

CHAPTER 2

The Right to Counsel

Chapter Preface

Case Overview: The 1963 case of *Gideon v. Wainwright* traveled an extraordinary path to reach the U.S. Supreme Court. In the original 1961 trial court, the defendant, Clarence Gideon, was accused of the theft of about $75 in cash and beverages from the Bay Harbor Poolroom in Panama City, Florida. He could not afford to pay an attorney to represent him and in court requested that one be appointed for him. Under the "special circumstances" test, the legal standard at that time, the lower court judge informed Gideon that he could appoint counsel only if Gideon were charged with a capital offense; that is, one carrying a possible death penalty. Gideon was found guilty and sentenced to five years in prison.

From prison Gideon requested that the Florida Supreme Court review his case, but his appeal was denied without a written opinion. Undeterred, Gideon went on to submit a handwritten request for review by the U.S. Supreme Court, asserting that his rights under the Constitution had been violated when the trial court failed to appoint him counsel. The Supreme Court granted his request in order to determine whether the case-by-case, special circumstances review standard should be changed.

Justice Hugo Black issued a majority opinion observing that the facts surrounding Gideon's conviction were so similar to the facts of the case where the special circumstances test was formulated—namely, *Betts v. Brady*—that the Court would have to overrule *Betts* in order to grant Gideon the right to counsel. Black then discusses the guarantee of counsel under the Sixth Amendment of the Constitution and whether this guarantee is a "fundamental principle of liberty and justice" and therefore applicable to state court action. Describing an earlier finding in *Powell v. Alabama*, Black concludes that the right to counsel must be seen as "fundamental and essential to a fair trial" and cannot be constitutionally denied. The Court therefore abandoned the special circumstances test and replaced it with the right to counsel for anyone accused of at least a felony. Based on these findings, Gideon's case was sent back to the trial court for a new trial where he could be represented by counsel.

In the new trial, Gideon's case seemed to justify the holding of the Supreme Court, since with the counsel of an attorney he was found not guilty. This result only further cemented the place of this landmark case, which has been described as the most celebrated Supreme Court decision of all time, in the American public's hearts and minds. The publication of a book about the trial and a subsequent movie also brought enormous media attention to this decision. Because of the equal access–equal justice philosophy underlying the case's logic, it is seen as a legal expression of the concerns of 1960s American society against a backdrop of civil rights protest and the women's rights movement.

Although the universal appeal of the *Gideon* decision has never been questioned, the practical application of the right to counsel has been difficult for the state and federal court systems. Appointing attorneys is expensive and as the number of indigent people accused of a crime continues to increase, the drain on the resources of the court system likewise increases. Additionally, social and political issues such as the treatment of prisoners of the war on terrorism have put a strain on the otherwise obvious nature of the right to counsel. The current "tough on crime" attitude of the American criminal justice system further lessens the availability of competent court-appointed representation. In the end, the ideals of *Gideon* have clashed with the cost to society of providing counsel to those who cannot afford to pay for their own, and so the struggle to balance these two competing interests continues.

> *"Even the intelligent and educated lay-*
> *man has small and sometimes no skill*
> *in the science of law."*

The Court's Opinion: The Right to Counsel Applies to the States and Is Fundamental to the Due Process of Law

Hugo Black

The Florida defendant Clarence Gideon was accused of breaking and entering a pool room with the intent to commit theft. At his trial, without sufficient funds to pay for a lawyer, Gideon requested that counsel be appointed to represent him. This request was denied since at the time only defendants facing capital (death-penalty) offenses were guaranteed counsel in the state of Florida. Gideon then represented himself and was found guilty and sentenced to five years in prison. Gideon argued to have his conviction overturned, based on the claim that the denial of counsel by the trial court had violated his right to counsel, as guaranteed by the Sixth Amendment. This right had been extended only to defendants in the federal court system up to that point. Upon review of Gideon's case, the Supreme Court found that the right to counsel was fundamental and should also apply to state court action. Justice Hugo Black wrote the opinion granting Gideon a new trial (at which Gideon was found not guilty). As a justice of the Supreme Court from 1937 to 1971, Black is the fourth-longest serving justice in the Court's history. He is noted for advocating a strict, literal interpretation of the Constitution.

Hugo Black, *Gideon v. Wainwright*, 372 US 335 (1963).

Since 1942, when *Betts v. Brady*, 316 U.S. 455, was decided by a divided Court, the problem of a defendant's federal constitutional right to counsel in a state court has been a continuing source of controversy and litigation in both state and federal courts. To give this problem another review here, we granted certiorari [agreed to hear the case]. Since Gideon was proceeding in forma pauperis [someone without funds and so entitled to pay no fees and have counsel appointed], we appointed counsel to represent him and requested both sides to discuss in their briefs and oral arguments the following: "Should this Court's holding in Betts v. Brady, 316 U.S. 455, be reconsidered?"

I.

The facts upon which Betts claimed that he had been unconstitutionally denied the right to have counsel appointed to assist him are strikingly like the facts upon which Gideon here bases his federal constitutional claim. Betts was indicted for robbery in a Maryland state court. On arraignment, he told the trial judge of his lack of funds to hire a lawyer and asked the court to appoint one for him. Betts was advised that it was not the practice in that county to appoint counsel for indigent defendants except in murder and rape cases. He then pleaded not guilty, had witnesses summoned, cross-examined the State's witnesses, examined his own, and chose not to testify himself. He was found guilty by the judge, sitting without a jury, and sentenced to eight years in prison.

Like Gideon, Betts sought release by habeas corpus, alleging that he had been denied the right to assistance of counsel in violation of the Fourteenth Amendment. Betts was denied any relief, and on review this Court affirmed. It was held that a refusal to appoint counsel for an indigent defendant charged with a felony did not necessarily violate the Due Process Clause of the Fourteenth Amendment, which, for reasons given, the Court deemed to be the only applicable federal constitutional provision. The Court said: "Asserted denial [of due process] is to be tested by an appraisal of the totality of facts in a given case. That which may, in one setting, constitute a denial of fundamental fairness, shocking to the universal sense of justice, may, in other circumstances, and in the light of other considerations, fall short of such denial."

Treating due process as "a concept less rigid and more fluid than those envisaged in other specific and particular provisions of the Bill of Rights," the Court held that refusal to appoint counsel under the particular facts and circumstances in the Betts case was not so "offensive to the common and fundamental ideas of fairness" as to amount to a denial of due process. Since the facts and circumstances of the two cases are so nearly indistinguishable, we think the *Betts v. Brady* holding if left standing would require us to reject Gideon's claim that the Constitution guarantees him the assistance of counsel. Upon full reconsideration we conclude that Betts v. Brady should be overruled.

II.

The Sixth Amendment provides, "In all criminal prosecutions, the accused shall enjoy the right . . . to have the Assistance of Counsel for his defence." We have construed this to mean that in federal courts counsel must be provided for defendants unable to employ counsel unless the right is competently and intelligently waived. Betts argued that this right is extended to indigent defendants in state courts by the Fourteenth Amendment. In response the Court stated that, while the Sixth Amendment laid down "no rule for the conduct of the States, the question recurs whether the constraint laid by the Amendment upon the national courts expresses a rule so fundamental and essential to a fair trial, and so, to due process of law, that it is made obligatory upon the States by the Fourteenth Amendment." In order to decide whether the Sixth Amendment's guarantee of counsel is of this fundamental nature, the Court in Betts set out and considered "[r]elevant data on the subject ... afforded by constitutional and statutory provisions subsisting in the colonies and the States prior to the inclusion of the Bill of Rights in the national Constitution, and in the constitutional, legislative, and judicial history of the States to the present date." On the basis of this historical data the Court concluded that "appointment of counsel is not a fundamental right, essential to a fair trial." It was for this reason the Betts Court refused to accept the contention that the Sixth Amendment's guarantee of counsel for indigent federal defendants was extended to or, in the words of that Court, "made obligatory upon the States by the Fourteenth Amendment." Plainly, had the Court concluded that appointment of counsel for an indigent criminal defendant was "a fundamental right, essential to a fair trial." it would have held that the Fourteenth Amendment requires appointment of counsel in a state court, just as the Sixth Amendment requires in a federal court.

We think the Court in Betts had ample precedent for acknowledging that those guarantees of the Bill of Rights which are fundamental safeguards of liberty immune from federal abridgment are equally protected against state invasion by the Due Process Clause of the Fourteenth Amendment. This same principle was recognized, explained, and applied in *Powell v. Alabama*, 287 U.S. 45 (1932), a case upholding the right of counsel, where the Court held that despite sweeping language to the contrary in *Hurtado v. California*, 110 U.S. 516 (1884), the Fourteenth Amendment "embraced" those "'fundamental principles of liberty and justice which lie at the base of all our civil and political institutions,'" even though they had been "specifically dealt with in another part of the federal Constitution." 287 U.S., at 67. In many cases other than *Powell* and *Betts*, this Court has looked to the fundamental nature of original Bill of Rights guarantees to decide whether the Fourteenth Amendment makes them obligatory on the States. Explicitly recognized to be of this "fundamental nature" and therefore made immune from state invasion by the Fourteenth, or some part of it, are the First Amendment's freedoms of speech, press, religion, assembly, association, and petition for redress of grievances. For the same reason, though not always in precisely the same terminology, the Court has made obligatory on the States the Fifth Amendment's command that private property shall not be taken for public use without just compensation, the Fourth Amendment's prohibition of unreasonable searches and seizures, and the Eighth's ban on cruel and unusual punishment. On the other hand, this Court in *Palko v. Connecticut*, 302 U.S. 319 (1937), refused to hold that the Fourteenth Amendment made the double jeopardy provision of the Fifth Amendment obligatory on the States. In so refusing, however, the Court, speaking through Mr. Justice Cardozo, was careful to emphasize that "immunities that are valid as against the federal government by force of the specific pledges of particular amendments have been found to be implicit in the concept of ordered liberty, and thus, through the Fourteenth Amendment, become valid as against the states" and that guarantees "in their origin . . . effective against the federal government alone" had by prior cases "been taken over from the earlier articles of the federal bill of rights and brought within the Fourteenth Amendment by a process of absorption."

We accept *Betts v. Brady*'s assumption, based as it was on our prior cases, that a provision of the Bill of Rights which is "fundamental and essential to a fair trial" is made obligatory upon the States by the Fourteenth Amendment. We think the Court in *Betts* was wrong, however, in concluding that the Sixth Amendment's guarantee of counsel is not one of these fundamental rights. Ten years before *Betts v. Brady*, this Court in *Powell v. Alabama*, after full consideration of all the historical data examined in *Betts*, had unequivocally declared that "the right to the aid of counsel is of this fundamental character." While the Court at the close of its *Powell* opinion did by its language, as this Court frequently does, limit its holding to the particular facts and circumstances of that case, its conclusions about the fundamental nature of the right to counsel are unmistakable. Several years later, in *Grosjean v. American Press Co.* in 1936, the Court reemphasized what it had said about the fundamental nature of the right to counsel in this language:

> "We concluded that certain fundamental rights, safeguarded by the first eight amendments against federal action, were also safeguarded against state action by the due process of law clause of the Fourteenth Amendment, and among them the fundamental right of the accused to the aid of counsel in a criminal prosecution."

And again in *Johnson v. Zerbst* in 1938 this Court said:

> "[The assistance of counsel] is one of the safeguards of the Sixth Amendment deemed necessary to insure fundamental human rights of life and liberty. . . . The Sixth Amendment stands as a constant admonition that if the constitutional safeguards it provides be lost, justice will not 'still be done.'"

In light of these and many other prior decisions of this Court, it is not surprising that the *Betts* Court, when faced with the contention that "one charged with crime, who is unable to obtain counsel, must be furnished counsel by the State," conceded that "[e]xpressions in the opinions of this court lend color to the argument. . . ." The fact is that in deciding as it did—that "appointment of counsel is not a fundamental right, essential to a fair trial"—the Court in *Betts v. Brady* made an abrupt break with its own well-considered precedents. In returning to these old precedents, sounder we believe than the new, we but restore constitutional principles established to achieve a fair system of justice. Not only these precedents but also reason and reflection require us to recognize that in our adversary system of criminal justice, any person hauled into court, who is too poor to hire a lawyer, cannot be assured a fair trial unless counsel is provided for him. This seems to us to be an obvious truth. Governments, both state and federal, quite properly spend vast sums of money to establish machinery to try defendants accused of crime. Lawyers to prosecute are everywhere deemed essential to protect the public's interest in an orderly society. Similarly, there are few defendants charged with crime, few indeed, who fail to hire the best lawyers they can get to prepare and present their defenses. That government hires lawyers to prosecute and defendants who have the money hire lawyers to defend are the strongest indications of the widespread belief that lawyers in criminal courts are necessities, not luxuries. The right of one charged with crime to counsel may not be deemed fundamental and essential to fair trials in some countries, but it is in ours. From the very beginning, our state and national constitutions and laws have laid great emphasis on procedural and substantive safeguards designed to assure fair trials before impartial tribunals in which every defendant stands equal before the law. This noble ideal cannot be realized if the poor man charged with crime has to face his accusers without a lawyer to assist him. A defendant's need for a lawyer is nowhere better stated than in the moving words of Mr. Justice Sutherland in *Powell v. Alabama:*

> "The right to be heard would be, in many cases, of little avail if it did not comprehend the right to be heard by counsel. Even the intelligent and educated layman has small and sometimes no skill in the science of law. If charged with crime, he is incapable, generally, of determining for himself whether the indictment is good or bad. He is unfamiliar with the rules of evidence. Left without the aid of counsel he may be put on trial without a proper charge, and convicted upon incompetent evidence, or evidence irrelevant to the issue or otherwise inadmissible. He lacks both the skill and knowledge adequately to prepare his defense, even though he have a perfect one. He requires the guiding hand

of counsel at every step in the proceedings against him. Without it, though he be not guilty, he faces the danger of conviction because he does not know how to establish his innocence."

The Court in *Betts v. Brady* departed from the sound wisdom upon which the Court's holding in *Powell v. Alabama* rested. Florida, supported by two other States, has asked that *Betts v. Brady* be left intact. Twenty-two States, as friends of the Court, argue that *Betts* was "an anachronism when handed down" and that it should now be overruled. We agree.

The judgment is reversed and the cause is remanded to the Supreme Court of Florida for further action not inconsistent with this opinion.

> *"An equalizing assistant is essential to
> ensure a balanced contest . . . and to
> provide the defendant with a fair
> opportunity to defend against the
> charges."*

The Right to Counsel Applies
Before, During, and After Trial

James J. Tomkovicz

*The following article discusses the central function of counsel be-
fore, during, and after trial and how the guarantee to counsel
under the Sixth Amendment has been interpreted to include all
of these phases. It notes that the* Gideon v. Wainwright *decision
was responsible for a shift from a case-by-case fact-based analysis as to the right to counsel to a guarantee of counsel for anyone
accused of a felony in a state proceeding. The article also examines the special case of the entering of a guilty plea and how
early state cases in this area, combined with the* Gideon *decision, mean that there is a general entitlement to counsel in the
plea-bargaining process. In short, the author concludes that there
is no time during the criminal prosecution phase that the presence of assistance is not required to ensure the rights of the accused.*

Originally, the trial was the sole battleground for the adversarial clash between the government and the individual charged with crime. There were no critical pretrial
events that could have significant effects on the outcome of a
criminal accusation. Moreover, post-trial efforts to overturn a

James J. Tomkovicz, from *The Right to The Assistance of Counsel: A Reference Guide
to the United States Constitution.* Westport, CT: Greenwood Press, 2002. Copyright ©
2002 by James J. Tomkovicz. All rights reserved. Reproduced by permission of Greenwood Publishing Group, Inc., Westport, CT.

guilty verdict—direct appeals of and collateral challenges to convictions—were not the norm. It is hardly surprising, therefore, that [as the Supreme Court stated in the 1973 case of *United States v. Ash*] that the Sixth Amendment's "core purpose . . . was to assure 'Assistance' *at trial*" (italics added). Through the past two centuries, the processes of adjudicating guilt or innocence have undergone significant expansions into both pretrial and post-trial periods. Nonetheless, in modern American systems of criminal justice, the trial remains the focal point and the most critical stage of the adversarial contest. Because the original intent of the Sixth Amendment's Framers was to afford legal representation during the confrontation with the state at trial, and because the trial remains the central event in the resolution of criminal accusations, there is no dispute that the Constitution affords an ample right to assistance of counsel at the trial in the courtroom. The Supreme Court opinions that have addressed questions of entitlement to assistance at pretrial or post-trial events have simply accepted the right to assistance *at trial* as a given.

In *Ross v. Moffitt* (1974), the Supreme Court said "the purpose of the trial stage from the State's point of view is to convert a criminal defendant from a person presumed innocent to one found guilty beyond a reasonable doubt." From the defendant's point of view, the object is to resist all prosecutorial efforts to dispel the presumption of innocence; that is, to prevent the state from satisfying its burden of proof by ensuring that the trier of fact has at least a reasonable doubt about guilt. At trial, both sides present evidence and arguments to the trier of fact in an effort to prevail on the merits. At trial, both society and the defendant have the most at stake. A loss for the state—a verdict of not guilty—will be final. No matter how flawed that decision is, no matter how strong the government's need to vindicate the public interest by trying the case again, the Fifth Amendment guarantee against "double jeopardy" will bar further pursuit of a conviction. On the other hand, a loss for the accused—a verdict of guilty—can have devastating impacts on his life and future. While a conviction is not necessarily final—a defendant can seek to overturn the verdict by appeal or collateral attack—the odds of securing a reversal of the finding of guilt are not favorable.

The Role of the Prosecutor

In the adversarial systems that all American jurisdictions adhere to, the government employs a prosecuting attorney to prove the guilt of the defendant. The prosecutor as explained in *Ross* "presents evidence to the court, challenges any witness offered by the defendant, argues rulings of the court, and makes direct arguments to the court and jury seeking to persuade them of the defendant's guilt." To defend against the state's charges and the prosecutor's efforts to establish their validity, the accused has the Sixth Amendment guarantee of a trained legal assistant. Defense counsel can present exculpatory evidence, challenge the state's case, make arguments, and seek to persuade the court and jury that the defendant is not guilty. The accused's right to the assistance of counsel at trial is unquestionable and unquestioned.

A trial ordinarily begins with jury selection and ends with a verdict. While the entitlement to a lawyer's assistance clearly extends to this entire period, it cannot be limited to that time frame without thwarting counsel's ability to serve her trial functions. Consequently, if a state were to restrict an accused's ability to retain representation to the formal trial itself or were to provide appointed counsel only for the actual trial process, it would undoubtedly violate the defendant's Sixth Amendment right to trial assistance. To be meaningful, the entitlement to assistance *at trial* must instead include the opportunity to have counsel's aid begin *before* the formal commencement of the trial in the courtroom. As decided in *Powell v. Alabama* (1932) counsel must be involved in the case sufficiently in advance to enable her to research the law and investigate the facts fully and to adequately prepare the best defense that she can. A lawyer cannot be expected to provide adequate equalization at the trial if she is not involved in a case until the actual beginning of the trial process. If the adversary system is to function fairly and achieve its ostensible ends, counsel must have adequate advance time to get ready to meet the state's evidence and arguments and present the defendant's side of the case. Perhaps it is best to speak of the core Sixth Amendment right as an entitlement to the assistance of counsel *for and at trial.*

The Right to Counsel Before Trial

In addition, modern American criminal justice systems afford opportunities to seek various sorts of judicial rulings prior to the formal commencement of a trial. A part of counsel's obligation to provide trial assistance is the responsibility to explore and present pretrial motions seeking rulings that promote the defendant's best interests. Pretrial motions can have substantial, sometimes determinative, impacts upon the outcome of the trial. Counsel, for example, might file a motion to suppress (i.e., to exclude from the trial) critical prosecution evidence, alleging that government officials obtained that evidence illegally. She might move to change venue if the atmosphere surrounding the trial suggests a community poisoned by prejudice, or she might seek to have the charges dismissed on constitutional or other grounds. Counsel might attempt to obtain pretrial rulings that defense evidence will be admissible at trial or that government evidence will be inadmissible under the rules of evidence. Appointed counsel might request additional state financial assistance to retain experts who will aid in constructing an adequate defense. For a variety of reasons, including efficiency, these and other pretrial motions are presented to the trial judge and resolved—sometimes after trial-like evidentiary hearings—before the process of selecting a jury and presenting evidence begins. Because of the important role that they play in resolving criminal accusations, pre-trial motions should be considered integral parts of the trial itself. Consequently, the right to assistance of trial counsel must include an entitlement to retained or appointed representation sufficiently before trial to enable counsel to research, prepare, and present pretrial motions, to resist prosecution motions contrary to the defendant's interests, and to provide zealous, effective representation at any hearings on these motions. The scope of the right to trial assistance must encompass an opportunity to have counsel involved in the defense well before the formal start of the trial process in the courtroom.

The Right to Counsel After Trial

Ordinarily, a trial ends with the return of a verdict and the entry of a judgment by the trial judge. In cases of conviction, defense counsel may attack the verdict by post-trial motion filed in the trial court. Complete legal assistance at trial may well include the preparation and presentation of various kinds of post-trial motions. Counsel, for example, might seek to have the judge enter a judgment of acquittal notwithstanding the jury's verdict, contending that no reasonable juror could have found guilt beyond a reasonable doubt from the evidence presented at trial. Alternatively, a defense attorney might argue that a conviction is unjust and against the weight of the evidence, [or] might claim that critical evidence supporting the conviction was improperly admitted at trial, or might assert that newly discovered, exculpatory evidence casts doubt upon the verdict. On these bases, counsel could request that the judge set aside the finding of guilt and order a new trial. The process of determining guilt or innocence—the trial process—is not completed until the trial judge rules on such post-trial motions. For right to counsel purposes, it seems logical and fair to view such post-trial proceedings as inseparable parts of the trial itself. Full enjoyment of the Sixth

Amendment's promise of trial assistance includes a right to representation for purposes of requesting the trial judge to overturn or set aside a verdict.

The Special Case of a Guilty Plea

The preceding discussion rests on the premise that an accused will stand trial before a judge or jury. In reality, many criminal accusations are resolved without trials. After negotiations with prosecutors, a very substantial percentage of those charged with offenses agree to forgo their entitlement to a trial and instead choose to enter a guilty plea. Two cases that predate the modern era of right to counsel jurisprudence provide support for a general right to assistance in guilty plea proceedings. In *Townsend v. Burke*, a 1948 case in which the accused pleaded guilty and was sentenced in the absence of counsel, the Supreme Court found a deprivation of due process and concluded that the conviction entered upon the plea could not stand. According to the Court, counsel "could have taken steps to see that the conviction . . . [was] not predicated on misinformation or misreading of court records, a requirement of fair play which absence of counsel withheld from this prisoner." In *Moore v. Michigan*, a 1957 case involving a guilty plea, the Supreme Court acknowledged that the "right to counsel is not a right confined to representation during the trial on the merits." It then held that due process of law afforded an entitlement to representation at the guilty plea proceeding in *Moore* because the defendant's "rights could not have been fairly protected without the assistance of counsel to help him with his defense." Because the accused did not have and did not properly waive counsel, the Court deemed his guilty plea "invalidly accepted" and reversed his conviction.

Both of these state court cases were decided at a time when a defendant's constitutional entitlement to appointed counsel in a state *trial* hinged upon a case-specific evaluation of the need for assistance. It is not surprising, therefore, that the findings of due process violations in *Townsend* and *Moore* were explicitly based on the specific facts of each case. Subsequently, however, in the landmark 1963 decision in *Gideon v. Wainwright*, the Supreme Court abandoned the case-by-case, "special circumstances" approach to deciding whether due process requires states to provide trial counsel for indigents. The *Gideon* Court instead ruled that all defendants charged with felonies are entitled to assistance at trial.

In the 1961 case of *Hamilton v. Alabama*, the Supreme Court stated that the "guiding hand of counsel is needed at the trial lest the unwary concede that which only bewilderment or ignorance could justify or pay a penalty which is greater than the law . . . exacts for the offense which they in fact and in law committed." When negotiations and a guilty plea proceeding substitute for and supplant the trial process, an accused has equally powerful interests in avoiding bewildered or ignorant concessions, in not paying penalties greater than the law exacts, and in having a process that comports with adversarial system principles of "fair play." The holding and reasoning of *Gideon*, coupled with the earlier holdings in *Townsend* and *Moore*, provide strong support for a general entitlement to counsel in the guilty plea process. Today, an accused surely has a constitutional right to legal assistance in a guilty plea proceeding whenever the charge is one that would require counsel at a trial.

Conclusions

In sum, in our adversary system the assistance of counsel at trial—the central event in the adjudication of guilt or innocence—is critical to ensure the fairness of the trial process. As observed by the Supreme Court in *U.S. v. Ash*, at no other juncture is the confrontation with "the intricacies of the law and the advocacy of the public prosecutor" more intense. No other phase of the process has a more critical impact upon the accused's fate. An equalizing assistant is essential to ensure a balanced contest, to guarantee a reliable search for truth, and to provide the defendant with a fair opportunity to defend against the charges. Thus, the need for such an assistant is greatest at trial. To fully satisfy this need, the accused must have an entitlement to assistance during the actual trial process, for a period of time prior to the formal start of the trial process, and for a period of time following the rendition of a verdict. An accused must also have an entitlement to assistance when he chooses to relinquish his right to a trial, electing instead to enter a guilty plea.

> *"We can celebrate the fact that the spark of* Gideon *is still alive and undoubtedly will be kept alive."*

The *Gideon* Decision Was Obvious

Judith S. Kaye

In this transcript of a speech given at a conference to commemorate the twenty-fifth anniversary of the Gideon *decision, a judge from the New York Court of Appeals discusses what the case meant to the legal profession at the time of its decision and its subsequent portrayal in the popular media. She goes on to relate why the facts of the case were the perfect example of what a competent defense attorney can do to change the outcome of a criminal case, citing specific court testimony. She concludes that although some charge that the principles of equal justice are dwindling, there is still much to celebrate in the decision: the enlightenment of the legal system to this basic right and the triumph of Clarence Gideon himself, a common man seeking to reverse an injustice.*

G ideon v. Wainwright has always held special significance for me because it was handed down the very week of my admission to the Bar of the State of New York. At the time I considered it a particularly thoughtful gesture on the part of the nine Justices of the United States Supreme Court to extend this unanimous welcome, and to assure me that I had chosen my livelihood well. Lawyers, declared Justice Black, are "necessities, not luxuries."

Judith S. Kaye, "Gideon v. Wainwright: A Lesson in the Obvious," *Pace Law Review*, vol. 10, spring 1990, pp. 419-22, 425-26. Reproduced by permission.

But the *Gideon* opinion, then as today, offered a brand new lawyer many serious lessons about the importance of the right to counsel, about the meaning of fairness and equal justice, and about the judicial process itself. It was remarkable in 1963, as it still is today, that a case that began with a habeas corpus petition written in pencil by an inmate at the Florida State Prison could end by toppling a Supreme Court precedent of two decades' standing and establishing a constitutional landmark that continues to this day to inspire the most profound dialogue about the fundamental nature of this nation's pledge of justice for all.

Gideon is a case that speaks to everyone. You don't have to be a lawyer to appreciate the plain good sense that motivated it. Professor Yale Kamisar recently referred to *Gideon v. Wainwright* as "one of the most popular decisions ever handed down by the United States Supreme Court." I don't know whether that is attributable more to Hugo Black or to the great talents of [writer] Anthony Lewis. It is some mark of the enduring popularity of *Gideon* that only recently I was able to buy another copy of [Lewis's] book *Gideon's Trumpet* at the SUNY-Albany campus bookstore, where it is required reading for the introductory political science course, and a copy of the movie for ten dollars at a drug store in the Colonie Mall, just outside Albany. And I don't know whether that is attributable more to Anthony Lewis or to the great talents of [actor] Henry Fonda.

Actually, every time I read the book or see the movie, as a character I seem to favor Fred Turner even over Clarence Gideon, or Abe Fortas, or the fabulous Velva Estelle Morris, Gideon's loyal landlady (played in the movie by Fay Wray, King Kong's friend). To be sure, Gideon, already a multiple loser, had uncommon persistence and Abe Fortas, already a multiple winner, had uncommon persuasiveness (as well as a lot of very good help). But it was Fred Turner, the Panama City trial lawyer—applying all the skills developed by advocates over years in the trenches—who singlehandedly drove home the point made by the Supreme Court in the *Gideon* opinion: that it is essential to a fair trial that defendants have effective counsel.

Fred Turner actually proved in a way everyone can understand that it's not just the rules of evidence and technical points of criminal law that require the assistance of a lawyer—though they surely do. He proved that you need a lawyer as much for the obvious things about a case as the arcane points of law. When Gideon at his first trial himself examined the operator of the Bay Harbor Poolroom—doing, in Justice Black's words in the decision "about as well as could be expected from a layman,"—he elicited testimony that some money, beer and wine had been stolen, and he left it at that. But it was Fred Turner in Gideon's second trial who picked up on that point and established exactly what was missing from the Bay Harbor Poolroom—twelve bottles of Coca-Cola, twelve cans of beer, four-fifths of wine and about $65 in change. Then he examined the cab driver, Preston Bray, who had driven Gideon downtown that fateful night:

Q: *Did he have any wine on him?*

A: No Sir.

Q: *Any Beer?*

A: No Sir.

Q: *Any Coca-Cola?*

A: No Sir.

Q: *Did his pockets bulge?*

A: No Sir.

In summation Turner then asked the jury three pointed questions:

What happened to the beer and the wine and the cokes? Mr. Gideon carried one hundred dollars' worth of change in his pocket? Do you believe that?

Well, they didn't. Why, I've often wondered, didn't that obvious point occur to anyone earlier? With Gideon having allegedly been under surveillance at all times, what had become of the proceeds of the theft? In his first trial, Gideon simply insisted that he was innocent, he didn't do any breaking and entering. That was the theme as well as the substance of his sterile examinations of witnesses and arguments to the jury, and it got him five years in state prison. He didn't know how to establish his innocence, and the state didn't lift a finger to help him. It took an experienced advocate dedicated to his client's interests to fashion Gideon's protestations of innocence into a story for the jury, a rationalization, a reasonable doubt that resulted in his acquittal. Until Gideon had a lawyer, no one else in the justice system had that function, or responsibility, or commitment.

If Fred Turner taught us the difficulty and importance of seeing the obvious, so did Hugo Black. In his *Gideon* opinion Justice Black expressed, simply and directly, the "obvious truth," the high principle that was immediately plain to everyone: "[I]n our adversary system of criminal justice," he said, "any person hauled into court, who is too poor to hire a lawyer, cannot be assured a fair trial unless counsel is provided for him. This noble ideal [of a fair trial] cannot be realized if the poor man charged with crime has to face his accusers without a lawyer to assist him." Indeed, looking at the simple good sense of those words, it's hard to think that the law ever allowed otherwise.

But Justice Black had struck that same blow for simple decency in just about the same words twenty years earlier, when he wrote that denial of the right to counsel in serious criminal cases defeats "the promise of our democratic society to provide equal justice under the law." Those words are taken from the dissent in *Betts v. Brady*, where the Supreme Court ruled six to three that the fourteenth amendment does *not* embody an inexorable command that an accused be afforded counsel. In the view of some, *Betts v. Brady* was outdated and wrong before the ink was dry on the option. It must have been an exquisite pleasure for Justice Black twenty years later in *Gideon* to announce for a unanimous Supreme Court: We agree.

As to *that* judgment I prefer a perception made by Clarence Gideon himself, in the extraordinary twenty-two page hand printed letter he had sent to Abe Fortas at the outset of their relationship. In Gideon's words, "each era finds an improvement in law; each year brings something new for the benefit of mankind. Maybe this will be one of those small steps forward." The *Gideon* case in 1963 represented exactly that sort of gradual improvement, advancement, evolution in thinking, and that's why—when the "obvious" was ultimately discovered by the Supreme Court—the decision immediately enjoyed such popularity among the legal profession, the press and the public. On the one hand it took a long time—far too long—to come to enlightenment. But on the other hand we did. . . .

A quarter of a century after *Gideon*, another truth has emerged as obvious. What was in 1963 such an expression of common sense decency that the public could immediately recognize and applaud it, has with time become clouded. We may still refer to the noble ideal that every defendant stands equal before the law, but in fact we have reconciled ourselves to standing short of achieving it. Ironically, with society and the law moving briskly toward a new century, there may well even be greater imbalances and distances between individuals like Clarence Gideon and acquittals after trial with effective counsel at defendants' side. The law grows increasingly sophisticated as public dedication to the principle of equal justice seems to dwindle.

So what's to celebrate, you ask. We can celebrate the fact that the spark of *Gideon* is still alive and undoubtedly will be kept alive by marking each anniversary, by collective and individual efforts to give meaning to its message, by courses that teach the "obvious truth" of *Gideon*. If the battle seems disheartening today, think what the odds must have looked like to Clarence Earl Gideon. Yet as *Gideon's Trumpet* describes, even as a five-time loser facing five years in the penitentiary a flame still burned in him. "He had not given up caring about life or freedom; he had not lost his sense of injustice."

[Lewis also recorded that] after the Supreme Court decision, a newspaper reporter asked Gideon, "Do you feel like you accomplished something?" He responded, "Well, I did."

Of course he did. He did and we will.

"Clarence Gideon, who died in 1972, would be disappointed today at the imperfect realization of his dream."

Gideon v. Wainwright Has Been Undermined

Anthony Lewis

By guaranteeing all criminal defendants counsel under the Sixth Amendment to the Constitution, particularly for those too poor to pay for legal representation, the Gideon *decision set a high standard for the criminal law system in the United States. In this article, Anthony Lewis, the author of the Pulitzer Prize–winning novelization of the case,* Gideon's Trumpet, *points out areas of conflict resulting from the decision in the present-day social and political climate. Lewis comments on the problems of lawyer incompetence in the ranks of public defenders and the lack of state funding and other resources earmarked to providing counsel. He also discusses the federal government's overriding aims of combating terrorism and how the war on terrorism jeopardizes the right to counsel. Ultimately, Lewis concludes that the states' court systems are failing to live up to the lofty judicial ideals expressed in the* Gideon *decision.*

Forty years ago, a poor, isolated prisoner in Florida, the least influential of Americans, wrote a letter to the Supreme Court—a letter in pencil, on lined prison paper—claiming that he had been wrongly denied the right to a lawyer when he was convicted. The Supreme Court agreed to

Anthony Lewis, "The Silencing of Gideon's Trumpet," *New York Times Magazine*, April 20, 2003, p. 50. Copyright © 2003 by The New York Times Company. Reprinted with permission.

hear his case and found that the Constitution required counsel to be provided in all serious criminal cases for defendants too poor to hire their own. Clarence Earl Gideon would have a new trial, this time with a lawyer.

The new jury found him not guilty: a happy ending not only for him but also for the principle that a lawyer's help is crucial for criminal defendants.

After the Supreme Court decision, I recognized that it would be, as I wrote then, "an enormous social task to bring to life the dream of *Gideon v. Wainwright*—the dream of a vast, diverse country in which every man charged with crime will be capably defended . . . sure of the support needed to make an adequate defense."

The Legacy of *Gideon v. Wainwright*

On this 40th anniversary, how have we done? I take my answer from a recent paper by Bruce Jacob, the lawyer who represented the State of Florida in the Supreme Court, arguing against Gideon's claim of a right to counsel. "I hoped that legislatures would meet the challenge," Jacob wrote. "That was at a time in my life when I still believed that legislators want to do the right thing. . . . The record of the courts in fulfilling the hopes represented by *Gideon* is a dismal one."

I was covering the Supreme Court [as a journalist] when it decided *Gideon v. Wainright*, and the case has always had special meaning for me. It is painful to hear Bruce Jacob express disappointment at today's courtroom inadequacies. Even more alarming is the assertion by the [George W.] Bush administration that in a whole new class of cases it can deny the right to counsel altogether. Those are the cases of American citizens designated by Bush as "enemy combatants."

One of them is José Padilla, born in Brooklyn in 1970 and arrested by federal agents [in May 2002] at O'Hare International Airport in Chicago. The administration claims that it can hold Padilla in solitary confinement indefinitely, without trial and without access to a lawyer.

Bruce Jacob's judgment rests on endless failures to bring the promise of *Gideon* to life. Many states and localities offer not even the minimal level of financial support needed for an adequate defense.

A Stressed System Peopled by Stressed Lawyers

And far too often the lawyers provided for indigent defendants have not met the barest standards of competence. Take the case of the sleeping lawyer. Calvin Burdine was on trial for his life in Texas when his appointed counsel, Joe Frank Cannon, fell asleep several times during the trial. The Texas Court of Criminal Appeals held that that was no reason to set aside Burdine's conviction. The United States Court of Appeals, considering the issue on habeas corpus, disagreed, but only by a vote of 9 to 5. That is, five of those distinguished federal judges thought a lawyer who fell asleep during a capital trial did not do enough harm to matter.

The truth of the proposition that a lawyer is essential was vividly demonstrated to me by something that happened in Gideon's second trial. Gideon had been charged with breaking and entering the Bay Harbor Poolroom in Panama City, Fla., in the early morning hours and taking some coins and wine. At his first trial, a taxi driver, Preston Bray, testified that Gideon had telephoned him and that he had gone to the poolroom and picked him up. When he got into the cab, Bray said, Gideon told him not to tell anyone about it. That was damaging testimony. And Gideon, without a lawyer, let it stand without any cross-examination.

In the second trial, Gideon had a lawyer: Fred Turner. After Preston Bray testified again that Gideon had told him not to say anything about picking him up that morning, Turner asked whether Gideon had ever said that to him before. The taxi driver answered, yes, Gideon said that every time he called a cab. "Why?" "I understand it was his wife—he had trouble with his wife."

Nothing could demonstrate more clearly the value of having a lawyer. But we know now that it has to be a competent lawyer. Fred Turner was competent, and then some. He not only destroyed the taxi driver's evidence against Gideon. He destroyed the chief prosecution witness, one Henry Cook, who said he had seen Gideon near the time of the break-in.

Turner suggested to the jury that it was really Cook himself who had committed the crime. He was in a good position to speak about Cook because he had represented Cook in two other cases.

Lawyers themselves bear some of the responsibility for the failures since the *Gideon* decision. Of the 13 people on death row in Illinois released between 1987 and 2000 after they were found innocent, four had been represented by lawyers who were later disbarred or suspended from practice. But so do the authorities who pick indifferent, sleepy, incompetent lawyers to defend men and women on matters as serious as life and death. Calvin Burdine's lawyer, Joe Frank Cannon, was appointed by judges in Houston to other cases after he slept through Burdine's trial. In Texas and other places, some appointments of counsel are regarded as sinecures [positions involving little to no work but providing a salary] to be given to friends and supporters.

Monetary Issues

Then there is the question of resources. Even a competent lawyer may not be able to mount an adequate defense against the state, with all its resources, if he has next to nothing for investigation and effectively works for starvation wages.

Bobby Houston spent 19 months in jail in Indianapolis without ever being tried, four of them after the charge against him, child molesting, had been dismissed. The public defender handling his case never told him, or told the prison authorities, about the dismissal.

We can surely say that Houston's lawyer lacked due diligence. But politics and money were also involved. At the time of the case, public defenders in Marion County, Ind.—working part time or more than part time—were paid $20,800 a year, plus $60 a month for all office expenses. They were so grossly underpaid and overworked that many could not even accept collect calls.

Why does the dream of the *Gideon* decision—the dream of a country in which every person charged with crime will be capably defended—remain just that, a dream? Why do judges countenance mockeries of legal representation? Why do we, the citizens, tolerate such unfairness? These are profound questions, and I can do no more than speculate on possible explanations.

One answer is plain. Criminal defendants and prisoners have little or no political power. Legislators see no votes in assigning competent lawyers for poor defendants or giving lawyers the resources to do their job properly. The Clarence Earl Gideons of this world are constituents who can safely be ignored. Many are barred from voting, and the rest seldom bother.

America's Hard-Line Attitude Toward Crime

There is more to it than defendants' and prisoners' lack of political power. This country differs from all other Western countries in its attitude toward crime and criminals. We are tough on crime, as the advocates of harsh measures put it. Critics might use a stronger term, like "brutal." American prisons tend to be more unpleasant than they are elsewhere; sentences, much longer.

And of course we impose the death penalty, which has been abandoned everywhere else in the trans-Atlantic world as a savage relic.

Why the United States takes so different a view of how to treat criminals is a question too deep for exploration here. But there is no doubt that the harsh view exists, exacerbated by politicians, starting with Richard Nixon and his "war on crime."

Manifestations of this harshness are widespread. The United States Court of Appeals for the Eighth Circuit recently approved the involuntary administration of antipsychotic drugs to a death-row inmate so he could be made sane enough to be executed. Then there was the prosecutor who argued that an execution should proceed even if the prisoner were to offer last-minute DNA evidence of his innocence.

DNA is at the center of an extraordinary recent development that sheds some light on attitudes toward criminal justice. The discovery of incompetence—or worse—at the Houston Police crime laboratory in recent months may affect hundreds of prosecutions in Harris County, where Houston is located, including many capital cases. More defendants from Harris County have been executed than from any other county in the United States. Now it turns out that the work of the laboratory is suspect.

What about the defense lawyers? Many simply did not have the resources to check the authenticity of the evidence that sent their clients to jail—or to death.

Among them were the lawyers for Josiah Sutton, convicted of rape [in 1999] and prosecuted in part on the basis of a DNA report from the Houston lab. After a Houston television station raised questions about the laboratory, the sample used to help convict Sutton was retested by an independent laboratory in Houston, which found that it did not match Sutton's DNA.

The case of Josiah Sutton and the Houston crime lab is one more proof of what Justice Black told us in *Gideon*: when the state brings its weight down on an individual, he or she cannot get justice without the help—the effective help—of a lawyer. That is a fundamental truth, an obvious truth, as Black said. But on the anniversary of the decision in *Gideon v. Wainwright*, that truth is being challenged in a way that I did not believe was possible in our country.

The Fight Against Terrorism and *Gideon*

In two cases now [i.e., in 2003] before the courts, Attorney General John Ashcroft is asserting that President Bush has the power to detain any American citizen indefinitely, in solitary confinement, without access to a lawyer, if he, the president, designates the detainee an "enemy combatant." The detainee cannot effectively challenge that designation. A court may hold a habeas corpus proceeding, but the government need produce only its own assertions of evidence, not subject to cross-examination. "Some evidence" will suffice—that is, any evidence, however unchecked and second-hand. That is the claim being made by the law officers of the United States.

I would not have believed that an attorney general would argue that an American could be held indefinitely without being able to speak to a lawyer. I seriously doubt that any attorney general in the years since *Gideon*, except the present occupant of the office, would have made that claim.

One of the pending cases concerns José Padilla, who became a gang member, was arrested half a dozen times and served several jail sentences. He became a Muslim. After traveling, in Pakistan among other places, Padilla flew into O'Hare Airport [on] May 8 [2002] and was arrested by federal agents. He was first detained as a material witness before a New York federal grand jury investigating the Sept. 11 terrorist attack on the World Trade Center. A judge appointed a lawyer for him and set a hearing for June 11. But on June 10 Ashcroft, who happened to be in Moscow, made a televised statement about Padilla. "We have captured a known terrorist," Ashcroft said. His arrest "disrupted an unfolding terrorist plot to attack the United States by exploding a radioactive 'dirty bomb.'" There has been no way for Padilla, or his lawyer, to challenge that statement, or for the news media to test its truth. It was a conviction by government announcement.

Padilla is confined in a Navy brig in South Carolina. The lawyer originally appointed to represent him in the material witness proceeding, Donna R. Newman, has been trying to see him—without success. A federal judge, Michael Mukasey, decided that she should have a chance to talk with him for the limited purpose of examining the evidence produced by the government in support of his designation as an "enemy combatant." But that decision was challenged anew by government lawyers.

They offered an affidavit by the director of the Defense Intelligence Agency, Vice Adm. Lowell E. Jacoby. He said successful interrogation of a prisoner depends largely on "creating an atmosphere of dependency and trust between the subject and interrogator. Developing the kind of relationship . . . necessary for effective interrogations . . . can take a significant amount of time. There are numerous examples of situations where interrogators have been unable to obtain valuable intelligence from a subject until months, or even years, after the interrogation process began." Admiral Jacoby said any access to counsel, however brief, "can undo months of work and may permanently shut down the interrogation process."

There is a certain paradox in Admiral Jacoby's affidavit. The very fact that extended interrogation in the absence of counsel may break a subject's will is one reason that the right to counsel is guaranteed in the criminal law. It is the basis of the Miranda rule.

Lack of Criminal Prosecution?

The government argues, and in the other "enemy combatant" case the United States Court of Appeals for the Fourth Circuit agreed, that the Sixth Amendment's guarantee of the right to counsel "in all criminal prosecutions" does not apply because

Padilla is not being prosecuted. In other words, the government can hold an American in prison for life without letting him see a lawyer if it takes care not to charge him with a crime and try him.[1] James Madison and the others who added the Sixth Amendment and the rest of the Bill of Rights to the Constitution in 1791 would surely have regarded that argument as sophistry.

Bruce Jacob has served on both the defense and the prosecution side of criminal justice. Forty years after *Gideon v. Wainwright* was decided, he takes a broad view of the constitutional right to counsel. It should include civil as well as criminal proceedings, he says in his paper: "The due process and equal protection clauses do not differentiate between criminal and civil cases." Paraphrasing Black's opinion, Jacob concludes: "Certainly any person haled into court or brought before any tribunal, whether criminal, civil or administrative . . . should, if indigent, be afforded counsel at public expense." With an eye on the enemy combatant cases, I would amend that statement to include any person deprived of his liberty by the state.

Clarence Earl Gideon was not a clear thinker, a man of the world or, least of all, an easy person to deal with. He was a petty criminal, a habitual one, worn out beyond his years by a difficult life. But he knew what he wanted. He turned down the first two lawyers offered him, when it came time for his second trial. He wanted Fred Turner, and that was a wise choice.

Fred Turner told Bruce Jacob that Gideon came to him with "a valise full of motions." Among other things, he wanted to move for a change of venue, to Tallahassee. Turner pointed out that he knew people in Panama City—in fact, he knew most of the jurors—but none in Tallahassee. Gideon agreed to drop the idea of a change of venue. Then Turner told him,

---

1. Padilla was ultimately charged with a crime in November 2005, although these charges were different than those alleged by Ashcroft. He was transferred in January 2006 to a federal prison in Miami, and his trial was scheduled for the fall of 2006.

"I'll only represent you if you will stop trying to be the lawyer and let me handle the case." Gideon agreed.

The Position of the Current Court

Clarence Gideon, who died in 1972, would be disappointed today at the imperfect realization of his dream. He would regret especially, I think, the failure of the Supreme Court to hold that the Constitution requires a meaningfully competent lawyer for the poor defendant—the court's countenancing, even in capital cases, of lawyers who scarcely go through the motions while their clients are convicted.

On the other hand, the Supreme Court has held fast to the principle that the right to consult a lawyer is, as Justice Black said, "fundamental." It is [now] a far more conservative court than the one that decided the *Gideon* case. . . . It has overruled or narrowed many precedents. But it has repeatedly reaffirmed its holding in *Gideon v. Wainwright*.

That is what makes the Bush administration's claim in the "enemy combatant" cases so extraordinary. Of course, José Padilla and the other man being held, Yasser Esam Hamdi, are not in precisely Gideon's position. They are not being prosecuted; they are being held indefinitely, without charges, in solitary confinement. They are not looking for counsel; they both already have lawyers, highly competent ones appointed by federal judges. But they are not allowed to talk to them. Those differences from Gideon's situation seem to make their need to consult the lawyers they have, if anything, more compelling.

The constitutional argument made by Ashcroft and his aides also seems imperfect. Perhaps the Sixth Amendment guarantee of counsel "in all criminal prosecutions" can be reasoned away as inapplicable to indefinite detention without charge, though I think the framers would have been astonished at the invention of a severe penalty for a suspect with fewer rights than he would have as a criminal defendant.

89

Due Process and Presidential Powers

But the Constitution also includes the Fifth Amendment. It provides that "no person shall . . . be deprived of life, liberty or property, without due process of law." José Padilla has been deprived of his liberty—forever, for all he knows. Has he had due process of law?

The Bush administration's answer to that question is essentially this: in a war against terrorism, any process that the president says is essential to the war is due process. Government lawyers argue that in wartime, courts must defer to the president's judgment.

The denial of counsel to José Padilla, then, is an aspect of something larger. About the time the *Gideon* case was decided, we began to hear about the imperial presidency. The terrorist attacks of Sept. 11, 2001, and now the war on Iraq have renewed that concept in even more extreme form. Bush has little trouble with a supine Congress. He wants the Constitution, too, as our judges enforce it, to yield to the supremacy of the president.[2]

2. The Supreme Court on April 3, 2006, ruled against Padilla, refusing to hear his appeal of a ruling that the Administration can hold a U.S. citizen in a military prison indefinitely and without charge.

"Gideon ... *may be about the illusion of justice and not the reality of it.*"

The Goal Set by the *Gideon* Decision Is Unrealistic

Nicholas Katzenbach

In the following article, Nicholas Katzenbach focuses on what is arguably the principal barrier to fulfilling the legal ideal of representation for all felony defendants: its cost to society. Katzenbach, a former U.S. attorney general under President Lyndon B. Johnson and now in private legal practice, argues that mere support of lawyers for defendants is not enough; the representation must be the same as if the accused could afford their own counsel. Because this level of counsel is expensive, it is not a popular idea. Katzenbach goes on to discuss the controversial role of the legal community in finding solutions to this problem and argues that donated time by attorneys is the only solution. In sum, although Gideon *may stand for equal access to representation with the assumed result of equal justice, society may be unwilling to pay the price in money and professional time to reach this lofty goal.*

Whether we are going to betray *Gideon* or whether we are really going to achieve all that *Gideon* stands for depends very much on what your vision of society is. What is the kind of society that we want to live in? The Court that decided *Gideon* and certainly people like Abe Fortas and Abe Krash [Gideon's lawyers in the case], had a vision of society, as I think did many in the 1960s—a vision that did not want

Nicholas Katzenbach, "Justice—A Reality or an Illusion," *Pace Law Review*, vol. 10, spring 1990, pp. 415-16. Reproduced by permission.

two societies, one rich and one poor. It did not want haves and have-nots when it so often turned out that the have nots were black.

So it seems to me it is important and not easy to try to think of what it is that we are celebrating in *Gideon*. Is it providing attorneys in criminal cases or is it a much broader concept? *Gideon* may be about obtaining access for everybody in our society to the system of justice that we have—that's a big job. Not an impossible job, but a big one. *Gideon*, however, may be about the illusion of justice and not the reality of it.

Why do I say that? Because it seems to me that people of almost any political faith agree that, in criminal cases, defendants ought to have lawyers. But what kind of representation are they meant to have? Most criminal defendants are guilty, so it isn't just a question, I assume, of making sure that you haven't picked up an innocent person in that net. If we want equal justice, we want people to have the same representation that they would have if they had money: vigorous representation whether they are guilty or whether they are innocent. I think it is at that point that a surprising number of people get off the boat. These people say, yes, they ought to have a lawyer but look at all the other things they want. They want expert testimony for example. Why give them all that? That costs money. And so, it is not really popular.

We also have civil legal services programs. These programs were initially enthusiastically supported. But they have become less popular. Bright young lawyers that joined these programs were viewed as troublemakers and therefore the programs became less popular. Many people in society, the governor of my state,[1] for example, will tell you that equal access isn't the problem of society; it is the problem of the lawyers. Lawyers

1. Katzenbach is refering to Thomas Kean, then the governor of New Jersey, who chaired the investigation into the 9/11 attacks.

ought to provide equal access, not other people. Lawyers ought to give their time. Other people should not have to give their money to achieve this.

Thus, it may be that what many in our society want *Gideon* to stand for is an illusion that there is equal access, that there is equal justice, when they are unwilling to pay the price to ensure that it actually occurs. I would say, therefore, that it is important to try and focus on what we want. No, *Gideon* is not going to be abandoned, but whether or not *Gideon* is betrayed or questioned or achieved is going to depend a good deal on what we want, and, perhaps even more, on what we are willing to pay for.

The Right to a Trial by Jury

Chapter Preface

Case Overview: In *Duncan v. Louisiana* (1968), the U.S. Supreme Court examined whether Gary Duncan, a nineteen-year-old African American in Louisiana, had been deprived of a right fundamental to the principles of liberty and justice when he was denied a jury trial for the charge of simple battery, an offense defined as the illegal touching of another without consent. Questions of discrimination complicated the case: Duncan was a relative of several black children who had recently been enrolled in a previously all-white school and the alleged battery occurred on a white child in an attempt to stop related unrest. A judge found Duncan guilty and sentenced him to jail time; Duncan appealed his case to the Louisiana Supreme Court, citing the right to a jury trial under the Sixth Amendment.

He argued that this section of the Bill of Rights, although literally applicable to only federal courts, should be applied to the state courts as well. The legal grounds for Duncan's argument was the so-called due process clause of the Fourteenth Amendment, which calls for due process of law before any loss of liberty. Thus, Duncan was arguing that the Sixth Amendment right to a jury trial should be inferred from the due process clause and should be applicable to state proceedings. The Louisiana court, adhering to its precedent of granting mandatory jury trials only for capital crimes, those where the death penalty can be applied or where imprisonment at hard labor could be imposed, denied review of the case.

Duncan then took his cause to the U.S. Supreme Court, which agreed to hear the case and issued a split decision.

Justice Byron White wrote the majority opinion of the Court, which held that the right to a jury trial was fundamental to principles of liberty and justice and thus should be applied to state action. He began the opinion with a review of the history of the jury trial in English and American courts. After observing the longstanding function of juries in balancing governmental power, he went on to disagree with a primary argument of the Louisiana court: that the crime was too minor to justify a jury. Refusing to draw a bright line, he stated that Duncan could have received up to two years for his offense and so this was sufficient loss of liberty to invoke the due process clause.

Justice John Marshall Harlan II authored the dissent in *Duncan*, appropriately, as Harlan had argued the opposing side to the majority's opinion in many previous cases, urging support for states' rights and the position that federal rights should not be imposed on states. Harlan stated that there were many fair ways to conduct a trial, and having a jury was not necessary for fundamental fairness. Further, he argued for states' autonomy in the way that they conduct their criminal prosecutions.

Like many Supreme Court cases in the 1950s and 1960s, however, *Duncan* reflected the ongoing racial strife associated with desegregation and the civil rights movement. The rampant prejudice and segregationist leadership of the Louisiana parish where Duncan was arrested may have been a factor in the case, and the decision thus became not only an interpretation of federal and state rights but a judicial statement about the need for desegregation and racial equality.

Although the *Duncan* decision was central to social upheaval at that time, questions about the role of juries are still being debated in recent times. For example, in the 2000 decision of *Apprendi v. New Jersey* the Supreme Court upheld the right to a jury in making decisions about criminal sentencing. Thus, the role of the jury in criminal cases, and therefore the role of society in the courtroom, continues to be shaped.

"Our conclusion is that in the American States, as in the federal judicial system, a general grant of jury trial for serious offenses is a fundamental right."

The Court's Majority Opinion: The Right to Trial by Jury Applies to State Actions

Byron White

Justice Byron White declares in the majority opinion of Duncan v. Louisiana *that trial by jury in criminal cases is fundamental to the American scheme of justice and therefore is a guaranteed right of the accused. The case concerned Gary Duncan, an older cousin of several black children recently transferred to a formerly all-white high school. Duncan was accused of battery, or illegal touching, of a white boy while breaking up a disagreement between the children. Tried by a judge, he was found guilty and sentenced to sixty days in prison and a $150 fine. Duncan appealed the verdict on the grounds that he was denied a trial by jury as guaranteed by the Sixth Amendment of the Constitution, and the Supreme Court agreed, with Justice White writing the majority opinion. White was a Supreme Court justice from 1962 to 1993.*

The Fourteenth Amendment denies the States the power to "deprive any person of life, liberty, or property, without due process of law." In resolving conflicting claims concerning the meaning of this spacious language, the Court has looked increasingly to the Bill of Rights for guidance; many of the

Byron White, majority opinion, *Duncan v. Louisiana*, 391 US 145 (1968).

rights guaranteed by the first eight Amendments to the Constitution have been held to be protected against state action by the Due Process Clause of the Fourteenth Amendment. That clause now protects the right to compensation for property taken by the State; the rights of speech, press, and religion covered by the First Amendment; the Fourth Amendment rights to be free from unreasonable searches and seizures and to have excluded from criminal trials any evidence illegally seized; the right guaranteed by the Fifth Amendment to be free of compelled self-incrimination; and the Sixth Amendment rights to counsel, to a speedy and public trial, to confrontation of opposing witnesses, and to compulsory process for obtaining witnesses.

The test for determining whether a right extended by the Fifth and Sixth Amendments with respect to federal criminal proceedings is also protected against state action by the Fourteenth Amendment has been phrased in a variety of ways in the opinions of this Court. The question has been asked whether a right is among those "'fundamental principles of liberty and justice which lie at the base of all our civil and political institutions,'" *Powell v. Alabama*, 287 U.S. 45, 67 (1932); whether it is "basic in our system of jurisprudence," *In re Oliver*, 333 U.S. 257, 273 (1948); and whether it is "a fundamental right, essential to a fair trial," *Gideon v. Wainwright*, 372 U.S. 335, 343–344 (1963); *Malloy v. Hogan*, 378 U.S. 1, 6 (1964); *Pointer v. Texas*, 380 U.S. 400, 403 (1965). The claim before us is that the right to trial by jury guaranteed by the Sixth Amendment meets these tests. The position of Louisiana, on the other hand, is that the Constitution imposes upon the States no duty to give a jury trial in any criminal case, regardless of the seriousness of the crime or the size of the punishment which may be imposed. Because we believe that trial by jury in criminal cases is fundamental to the American scheme of justice, we hold that the Fourteenth Amendment guarantees a right of jury trial in all criminal cases which—

were they to be tried in a federal court—would come within the Sixth Amendment's guarantee. Since we consider the appeal before us to be such a case, we hold that the Constitution was violated when appellant's demand for jury trial was refused.

The Historical Basis

The history of trial by jury in criminal cases has been frequently told. It is sufficient for present purposes to say that by the time our Constitution was written, jury trial in criminal cases had been in existence in England for several centuries and carried impressive credentials traced by many to Magna Carta. Its preservation and proper operation as a protection against arbitrary rule were among the major objectives of the revolutionary settlement which was expressed in the Declaration and Bill of Rights of 1689. In the 18th century [legal scholar William] Blackstone could write:

> Our law has therefore wisely placed this strong and two-fold barrier, of a presentment and a trial by jury, between the liberties of the people and the prerogative of the crown. It was necessary, for preserving the admirable balance of our constitution, to vest the executive power of the laws in the prince: and yet this power might be dangerous and destructive to that very constitution, if exerted without check or control, by justices of oyer and terminer ["to hear and determine"] occasionally named by the crown; who might then, as in France or Turkey, imprison, dispatch, or exile any man that was obnoxious to the government, by an instant declaration that such is their will and pleasure. But the founders of the English law have, with excellent forecast, contrived that ... the truth of every accusation, whether preferred in the shape of indictment, information, or appeal, should afterwards be confirmed by the unanimous suffrage of twelve of his equals and neighbours, indifferently chosen and superior to all suspicion.

Jury trial came to America with English colonists, and received strong support from them. Royal interference with the jury trial was deeply resented. Among the resolutions adopted by the First Congress of the American Colonies (the Stamp Act Congress) on October 19, 1765—resolutions deemed by their authors to state "the most essential rights and liberties of the colonists"—was the declaration:

> "That trial by jury is the inherent and invaluable right of every British subject in these colonies."

The First Continental Congress, in the resolve of October 14, 1774, objected to trials before judges dependent upon the Crown alone for their salaries and to trials in England for alleged crimes committed in the colonies; the Congress therefore declared:

> "That the respective colonies are entitled to the common law of England, and more especially to the great and inestimable privilege of being tried by their peers of the vicinage [local area], according to the course of that law."

The Declaration of Independence stated solemn objections to the King's making "Judges dependent on his Will alone, for the tenure of their offices, and the amount and payment of their salaries," to his "depriving us in many cases, of the benefits of Trial by Jury," and to his "transporting us beyond Seas to be tried for pretended offenses." The Constitution itself, in Art. III, 2, commanded:

> "The Trial of all Crimes, except in Cases of Impeachment, shall be by Jury; and such Trial shall be held in the State where the said Crimes shall have been committed."

Objections to the Constitution because of the absence of a bill of rights were met by the immediate submission and adoption of the Bill of Rights. Included was the Sixth Amendment which, among other things, provided:

"In all criminal prosecutions, the accused shall enjoy the right to a speedy and public trial, by an impartial jury of the State and district wherein the crime shall have been committed."

The constitutions adopted by the original States guaranteed jury trial. Also, the constitution of every State entering the Union thereafter in one form or another protected the right to jury trial in criminal cases.

Even such skeletal history is impressive support for considering the right to jury trial in criminal cases to be fundamental to our system of justice, an importance frequently recognized in the opinions of this Court. For example, the Court has said:

"Those who emigrated to this country from England brought with them this great privilege 'as their birthright and inheritance, as a part of that admirable common law which had fenced around and interposed barriers on every side against the approaches of arbitrary power.'"

Jury trial continues to receive strong support. The laws of every State guarantee a right to jury trial in serious criminal cases; no State has dispensed with it; nor are there significant movements underway to do so. Indeed, the three most recent state constitutional revisions, in Maryland, Michigan, and New York, carefully preserved the right of the accused to have the judgment of a jury when tried for a serious crime.

Contrary Prior Cases

We are aware of prior cases in this Court in which the prevailing opinion contains statements contrary to our holding today that the right to jury trial in serious criminal cases is a fundamental right and hence must be recognized by the States as part of their obligation to extend due process of law to all persons within their jurisdiction. Louisiana relies especially on *Maxwell v. Dow*, 176 U.S. 581 (1900); *Palko v. Connecticut*, 302

U.S. 319 (1937); and *Snyder v. Massachusetts*, 291 U.S. 97 (1934). None of these cases, however, dealt with a State which had purported to dispense entirely with a jury trial in serious criminal cases. *Maxwell* held that no provision of the Bill of Rights applied to the States—a position long since repudiated—and that the Due Process Clause of the Fourteenth Amendment did not prevent a State from trying a defendant for a noncapital offense with fewer than 12 men on the jury. It did not deal with a case in which no jury at all had been provided. In neither *Palko* nor *Snyder* was jury trial actually at issue, although both cases contain important dicta [statements] asserting that the right to jury trial is not essential to ordered liberty and may be dispensed with by the States regardless of the Sixth and Fourteenth Amendments. These observations, though weighty and respectable, are nevertheless dicta, unsupported by holdings in this Court that a State may refuse a defendant's demand for a jury trial when he is charged with a serious crime. Perhaps because the right to jury trial was not directly at stake, the Court's remarks about the jury in *Palko* and *Snyder* took no note of past or current developments regarding jury trials, did not consider its purposes and functions, attempted no inquiry into how well it was performing its job, and did not discuss possible distinctions between civil and criminal cases. In *Malloy v. Hogan*, supra [as cited above], the Court rejected *Palko's* discussion of the self-incrimination clause. Respectfully, we reject the prior dicta regarding jury trial in criminal cases.

The guarantees of jury trial in the Federal and State Constitutions reflect a profound judgment about the way in which law should be enforced and justice administered. A right to jury trial is granted to criminal defendants in order to prevent oppression by the Government.

How Juries Protect Rights

Those who wrote our constitutions knew from history and experience that it was necessary to protect against unfounded criminal charges brought to eliminate enemies and against judges too responsive to the voice of higher authority. The framers of the constitutions strove to create an independent judiciary but insisted upon further protection against arbitrary action. Providing an accused with the right to be tried by a jury of his peers gave him an inestimable safeguard against the corrupt or overzealous prosecutor and against the compliant, biased, or eccentric judge. If the defendant preferred the common-sense judgment of a jury to the more tutored but perhaps less sympathetic reaction of the single judge, he was to have it. Beyond this, the jury trial provisions in the Federal and State Constitutions reflect a fundamental decision about the exercise of official power—a reluctance to entrust plenary powers over the life and liberty of the citizen to one judge or to a group of judges. Fear of unchecked power, so typical of our State and Federal Governments in other respects, found expression in the criminal law in this insistence upon community participation in the determination of guilt or innocence. The deep commitment of the Nation to the right of jury trial in serious criminal cases as a defense against arbitrary law enforcement qualifies for protection under the Due Process Clause of the Fourteenth Amendment, and must therefore be respected by the States.

Of course jury trial has "its weaknesses and the potential for misuse," *Singer v. United States*, 380 U.S. 24, 35 (1965). We are aware of the long debate, especially in this [the twentieth] century, among those who write about the administration of justice, as to the wisdom of permitting untrained laymen to determine the facts in civil and criminal proceedings. Although the debate has been intense, with powerful voices on either side, most of the controversy has centered on the jury in civil cases. Indeed, some of the severest critics of civil juries acknowledge that the arguments for criminal juries are much stronger. In addition, at the heart of the dispute have been express or implicit assertions that juries are incapable of adequately understanding evidence or determining issues of fact, and that they are unpredictable, quixotic, and little better than a roll of dice. Yet the most recent and exhaustive study of the jury in criminal cases concluded that juries do understand the evidence and come to sound conclusions in most of the cases presented to them and that when juries differ with the result at which the judge would have arrived, it is usually because they are serving some of the very purposes for which they were created and for which they are now employed.

Jury Trials Are a Fundmental Right

The State of Louisiana urges that holding that the Fourteenth Amendment assures a right to jury trial will cast doubt on the integrity of every trial conducted without a jury. Plainly, this is not the import of our holding. Our conclusion is that in the American States, as in the federal judicial system, a general grant of jury trial for serious offenses is a fundamental right, essential for preventing miscarriages of justice and for assuring that fair trials are provided for all defendants. We would not assert, however, that every criminal trial—or any particular trial—held before a judge alone is unfair or that a defendant may never be as fairly treated by a judge as he would be by a jury. Thus we hold no constitutional doubts about the practices, common in both federal and state courts, of accepting waivers of jury trial and prosecuting petty crimes without extending a right to jury trial. However, the fact is that in most places more trials for serious crimes are to juries than to a court alone; a great many defendants prefer the judgment of a jury to that of a court. Even where defendants are satisfied with bench trials, the right to a jury trial very likely serves its intended purpose of making judicial or prosecutorial unfairness less likely.

A Petty Crime?

Louisiana's final contention is that even if it must grant jury trials in serious criminal cases, the conviction before us is valid and constitutional because here the petitioner was tried for simple battery and was sentenced to only 60 days in the parish prison. We are not persuaded. It is doubtless true that there is a category of petty crimes or offenses which is not subject to the Sixth Amendment jury trial provision and should not be subject to the Fourteenth Amendment jury trial requirement here applied to the States. Crimes carrying possible penalties up to six months do not require a jury trial if they otherwise qualify as petty offenses, *Cheff v. Schnackenberg*, 384 U.S. 373 (1966). But the penalty authorized for a particular crime is of major relevance in determining whether it is serious or not and may in itself, if severe enough, subject the trial to the mandates of the Sixth Amendment, *District of Columbia v. Clawans*, 300 U.S. 617 (1937). The penalty authorized by the law of the locality may be taken "as a gauge of its social and ethical judgments," 300 U.S., at 628, of the crime in question. In *Clawans* the defendant was jailed for 60 days, but it was the 90-day authorized punishment on which the Court focused in determining that the offense was not one for which the Constitution assured trial by jury. In the case before us the Legislature of Louisiana has made simple battery a criminal offense punishable by imprisonment for up to two years and a fine. The question, then, is whether a crime carrying such a penalty is an offense which Louisiana may insist on trying without a jury.

We think not. So-called petty offenses were tried without juries both in England and in the Colonies and have always been held to be exempt from the otherwise comprehensive language of the Sixth Amendment's jury trial provisions. There is no substantial evidence that the Framers intended to depart from this established common-law practice, and the possible consequences to defendants from convictions for petty offenses have been thought insufficient to outweigh the benefits to efficient law enforcement and simplified judicial administration resulting from the availability of speedy and inexpensive nonjury adjudications. These same considerations compel the same result under the Fourteenth Amendment. Of course the boundaries of the petty offense category have always been ill-defined, if not ambulatory [movable]. In the absence of an explicit constitutional provision, the definitional task necessarily falls on the courts, which must either pass upon the validity of legislative attempts to identify those petty offenses which are exempt from jury trial or, where the legislature has not addressed itself to the problem, themselves face the question in the first instance. In either case it is necessary to draw a line in the spectrum of crime, separating petty from serious infractions. This process, although essential, cannot be wholly satisfactory, for it requires attaching different consequences to events which, when they lie near the line, actually, differ very little.

Laws and Practices in the Nation

In determining whether the length of the authorized prison term or the seriousness of other punishment is enough in itself to require a jury trial, we are counseled by *District of Columbia v. Clawans*, supra, to refer to objective criteria, chiefly the existing laws and practices in the Nation. In the federal system, petty offenses are defined as those punishable by no more than six months in prison and a $500 fine. In 49 of the 50 States crimes subject to trial without a jury, which occasionally include simple battery, are punishable by no more than one year in jail. Moreover, in the late 18th century in America crimes triable without a jury were for the most part punishable by no more than a six-month prison term, although there appear to have been exceptions to this rule. We need not, however, settle in this case the exact location of the line between petty offenses and serious crimes. It is sufficient for our purposes to hold that a crime punishable by two years in prison is, based on past and contemporary standards in this country, a serious crime and not a petty offense. Consequently, appellant was entitled to a jury trial and it was error to deny it.

The judgment below is reversed and the case is remanded for proceedings not inconsistent with this opinion.

| "It simply has not been demonstrated, nor, I think, can it be demonstrated, that trial by jury is the only fair means of resolving issues of fact."

The Court's Dissenting Opinion: A Jury Trial Is Not Required for Due Process of Law

John Marshall Harlan II

In his dissenting opinion in Duncan v. Louisiana, *Justice John Marshall Harlan II argues that just because a trial by jury is an institution of the American justice system does not mean it should be guaranteed in all cases by the Constitution. He disagrees with the subjugation of the Sixth Amendment of the Bill of Rights to the due process clause of the Fourteenth Amendment, thus making the guarantee of a jury trial applicable to state actions. Instead, he would prefer that states maintained the freedom to try accused criminals according to their individual state laws. He particularly disagrees with the Court's continuing right-by-right analysis of whether sections of the Bill of Rights apply to the states (as opposed to a complete application or nonapplication). Further, he states that the simple battery charge of this case is not a sufficiently serious crime to justify trial by jury.*

Every American jurisdiction provides for trial by jury in criminal cases. The question before us is not whether jury trial is an ancient institution, which it is; nor whether it plays

John Marshall Harlan II, dissenting opinion, *Duncan v. Louisiana*, 391 US 145 (1968).

a significant role in the administration of criminal justice, which it does; nor whether it will endure, which it shall. The question in this case is whether the State of Louisiana, which provides trial by jury for all felonies, is prohibited by the Constitution from trying charges of simple battery to the court alone. In my view, the answer to that question, mandated alike by our constitutional history and by the longer history of trial by jury, is clearly "no."

The States have always borne primary responsibility for operating the machinery of criminal justice within their borders, and adapting it to their particular circumstances. In exercising this responsibility, each State is compelled to conform its procedures to the requirements of the Federal Constitution. The Due Process Clause of the Fourteenth Amendment requires that those procedures be fundamentally fair in all respects. It does not, in my view, impose or encourage nationwide uniformity for its own sake; it does not command adherence to forms that happen to be old; and it does not impose on the States the rules that may be in force in the federal courts except where such rules are also found to be essential to basic fairness.

The Court's approach to this case is an uneasy and illogical compromise among the views of various Justices on how the Due Process Clause should be interpreted. The Court does not say that those who framed the Fourteenth Amendment intended to make the Sixth Amendment applicable to the States. And the Court concedes that it finds nothing unfair about the procedure by which the present appellant was tried. Nevertheless, the Court reverses its conviction: it holds, for some reason not apparent to me, that the Due Process Clause incorporates the particular clause of the Sixth Amendment that requires trial by jury in federal criminal cases—including, as I read its opinion, the sometimes trivial accompanying baggage of judicial interpretation in federal contexts.

I have raised my voice many times before against the Court's continuing undiscriminating insistence upon fastening on the States federal notions of criminal justice, and I must do so again in this instance. With all respect, the Court's approach and its reading of history are altogether topsy-turvy.

The Role of the Bill of Rights

I believe I am correct in saying that every member of the Court for at least the last 135 years has agreed that our Founders did not consider the requirements of the Bill of Rights so fundamental that they should operate directly against the States. They were wont to believe rather that the security of liberty in America rested primarily upon the dispersion of governmental power across a federal system. The Bill of Rights was considered unnecessary by some but insisted upon by others in order to curb the possibility of abuse of power by the strong central government they were creating.

The Civil War Amendments dramatically altered the relation of the Federal Government to the States. The first section of the Fourteenth Amendment imposes highly significant restrictions on state action. But the restrictions are couched in very broad and general terms: citizenship; privileges and immunities; due process of law; equal protection of the laws. Consequently, for 100 years this Court has been engaged in the difficult process Professor [Louis L.] Jaffe has well called "the search for intermediate premises." The question has been, Where does the Court properly look to find the specific rules that define and give content to such terms as "life, liberty, or property" and "due process of law"?

A few members of the Court have taken the position that the intention of those who drafted the first section of the Fourteenth Amendment was simply, and exclusively, to make the provisions of the first eight Amendments applicable to state action. This view has never been accepted by this Court. In my view, often expressed elsewhere, the first section of the

Fourteenth Amendment was meant neither to incorporate, nor to be limited to, the specific guarantees of the first eight Amendments. The overwhelming historical evidence marshalled by Professor [Charles] Fairman demonstrates to me conclusively that the Congressmen and state legislators who wrote, debated, and ratified the Fourteenth Amendment did not think they were "incorporating" the Bill of Rights, and the very breadth and generality of the Amendment's provisions suggest that its authors did not suppose that the Nation would always be limited to mid-19th century conceptions of "liberty" and "due process of law" but that the increasing experience and evolving conscience of the American people would add new "intermediate premises." In short, neither history, nor sense, supports using the Fourteenth Amendment to put the States in a constitutional straitjacket with respect to their own development in the administration of criminal or civil law.

Although I therefore fundamentally disagree with the total incorporation view of the Fourteenth Amendment, it seems to me that such a position does at least have the virtue, lacking in the Court's selective incorporation approach, of internal consistency: we look to the Bill of Rights, word for word, clause for clause, precedent for precedent because, it is said, the men who wrote the Amendment wanted it that way. For those who do not accept this "history," a different source of "intermediate premises" must be found. The Bill of Rights is not necessarily irrelevant to the search for guidance in interpreting the Fourteenth Amendment, but the reason for and the nature of its relevance must be articulated. . . .

Rejecting Total Incorporation

Today's Court still remains unwilling to accept the total-incorporationists' view of the history of the Fourteenth Amendment. This, if accepted, would afford a cogent reason for applying the Sixth Amendment to the States. The Court is also, apparently, unwilling to face the task of determining whether denial of trial by jury in the situation before us, or in other situations, is fundamentally unfair. Consequently, the Court has compromised on the ease of the incorporationist position, without its internal logic. It has simply assumed that the question before us is whether the Jury Trial Clause of the Sixth Amendment should be incorporated into the Fourteenth, jot-for-jot and case-for-case, or ignored. Then the Court merely declares that the clause in question is "in" rather than "out."

Defining Fundamental Fairness

The Court has justified neither its starting place nor its conclusion. If the problem is to discover and articulate the rules of fundamental fairness in criminal proceedings, there is no reason to assume that the whole body of rules developed in this Court constituting Sixth Amendment jury trial must be regarded as a unit. The requirement of trial by jury in federal criminal cases has given rise to numerous subsidiary questions respecting the exact scope and content of the right. It surely cannot be that every answer the Court has given, or will give, to such a question is attributable to the Founders; or even that every rule announced carries equal conviction of this Court; still less can it be that every such subprinciple is equally fundamental to ordered liberty.

Examples abound. I should suppose it obviously fundamental to fairness that a "jury" means an "impartial jury." I should think it equally obvious that the rule, imposed long ago in the federal courts, that "jury" means "jury of exactly twelve," is not fundamental to anything: there is no significance except to mystics in the number 12. Again, trial by jury has been held to require a unanimous verdict of jurors in the federal courts, although unanimity has not been found essential to liberty in Britain, where the requirement has been abandoned.

One further example is directly relevant here. The co-existence of a requirement of jury trial in federal criminal cases and a historic and universally recognized exception for "petty crimes" has compelled this Court, on occasion, to decide whether a particular crime is petty, or is included within the guarantee. Individual cases have been decided without great conviction and without reference to a guiding principle. The Court today holds, for no discernible reason, that if and when the line is drawn its exact location will be a matter of such fundamental importance that it will be uniformly imposed on the States. This Court is compelled to decide such obscure borderline questions in the course of administering federal law. This does not mean that its decisions are demonstrably sounder than those that would be reached by state courts and legislatures, let alone that they are of such importance that fairness demands their imposition throughout the Nation.

Even if I could agree that the question before us is whether Sixth Amendment jury trial is totally "in" or totally "out," I can find in the Court's opinion no real reasons for concluding that it should be "in." The basis for differentiating among clauses in the Bill of Rights cannot be that only some clauses are in the Bill of Rights, or that only some are old and much praised, or that only some have played an important role in the development of federal law. These things are true of all. The Court says that some clauses are more "fundamental" than others, but it turns out to be using this word in a sense that would have astonished Mr. Justice [Benjamin] Cardozo and which, in addition, is of no help. The word does not mean "analytically critical to procedural fairness" for no real analysis of the role of the jury in making procedures fair is even attempted. Instead, the word turns out to mean "old," "much praised," and "found in the Bill of Rights." The definition of "fundamental" thus turns out to be circular.

Applying the Ideals to *Duncan*

Since, as I see it, the Court has not even come to grips with the issues in this case, it is necessary to start from the beginning. When a criminal defendant contends that his state conviction lacked "due process of law," the question before this Court, in my view, is whether he was denied any element of fundamental procedural fairness. Believing, as I do, that due process is an evolving concept and that old principles are subject to re-evaluation in light of later experience, I think it appropriate to deal on its merits with the question whether Louisiana denied appellant due process of law when it tried him for simple assault without a jury.

The obvious starting place is the fact that this Court has, in the past, held that trial by jury is not a requisite of criminal due process. . . .

Although it is of course open to this Court to reexamine these decisions, I can see no reason why they should now be overturned. It can hardly be said that time has altered the question, or brought significant new evidence to bear upon it. The virtues and defects of the jury system have been hotly debated for a long time, and are hotly debated today, without significant change in the lines of argument.

A Jury Is Not Required for Due Process

The argument that jury trial is not a requisite of due process is quite simple. The central proposition of *Palko* [*v. Connecticut*], a proposition to which I would adhere, is that "due process of law" requires only that criminal trials be fundamentally fair. As stated above, apart from the theory that it was historically intended as a mere shorthand for the Bill of Rights, I do not see what else "due process of law" can intelligibly be thought to mean. If due process of law requires only fundamental fairness, then the inquiry in each case must be whether a state trial process was a fair one. The Court has held, properly I think, that in an adversary process it is a requisite of fairness, for which there is no adequate substitute, that a criminal defendant be afforded a right to counsel and to cross-examine opposing witnesses. But it simply has not been demonstrated, nor, I think, can it be demonstrated, that trial by jury is the only fair means of resolving issues of fact.

The jury is of course not without virtues. It affords ordinary citizens a valuable opportunity to participate in a process of government, an experience fostering, one hopes, a respect for law. It eases the burden on judges by enabling them to share a part of their sometimes awesome responsibility. A jury may, at times, afford a higher justice by refusing to enforce harsh laws (although it necessarily does so haphazardly, raising the questions whether arbitrary enforcement of harsh laws is better than total enforcement, and whether the jury system is to be defended on the ground that jurors sometimes disobey their oaths). And the jury may, or may not, contribute desirably to the willingness of the general public to accept criminal judgments as just.

It can hardly be gainsaid, however, that the principal original virtue of the jury trial—the limitations a jury imposes on a tyrannous judiciary—has largely disappeared. We no longer live in a medieval or colonial society. Judges enforce laws enacted by democratic decision, not by regal fiat. They are elected by the people or appointed by the people's elected officials, and are responsible not to a distant monarch alone but to reviewing courts, including this one.

The jury system can also be said to have some inherent defects, which are multiplied by the emergence of the criminal law from the relative simplicity that existed when the jury system was devised. It is a cumbersome process, not only imposing great cost in time and money on both the State and the jurors themselves, but also contributing to delay in the machinery of justice. Untrained jurors are presumably less adept at reaching accurate conclusions of fact than judges, particularly if the issues are many or complex. And it is argued by some that trial by jury, far from increasing public respect for law, impairs it: the average man, it is said, reacts favorably neither to the notion that matters he knows to be complex are being decided by other average men, nor to the way the jury system distorts the process of adjudication. . . .

Support State Experimentation

In sum, there is a wide range of views on the desirability of trial by jury, and on the ways to make it most effective when it is used; there is also considerable variation from State to State in local conditions such as the size of the criminal caseload, the ease or difficulty of summoning jurors, and other trial conditions bearing on fairness. We have before us, therefore, an almost perfect example of a situation in which the celebrated dictum of Mr. Justice [Louis] Brandeis should be invoked. It is, he said,

> "one of the happy incidents of the federal system that a single courageous State may, if its citizens choose, serve as a laboratory. . . ." *New State Ice Co. v. Liebmann*, 285 U.S. 262, 280, 311 (dissenting opinion).

This Court, other courts, and the political process are available to correct any experiments in criminal procedure that prove fundamentally unfair to defendants. That is not what is being done today: instead, and quite without reason, the Court has chosen to impose upon every State one means of trying criminal cases; it is a good means, but it is not the only fair means, and it is not demonstrably better than the alternatives States might devise.

I would affirm the judgment of the Supreme Court of Louisiana.

"No matter how laws were enacted and no matter how judges obtained and retained office, Americans saw a need to check judicial power. Juries could help do this."

Trial by Jury Is a Check Against Abuses of Power

Randolph N. Jonakait

The jury has long held a central role in the American judicial system, helping to balance the inherent power of judges and other governmental officials. Particularly in criminal matters, the jury brings society's views about how laws should be applied and enforced into the courtroom and into practice. In the following article, New York law professor Randolph N. Jonakait examines this "checks and balances" function of the American jury. He discusses the place of Duncan v. Louisiana *in ensuring that juries continue to play this important role, particularly during times of social unrest. Jonakait concludes that as expected, when juries and judges disagree, the jury is most likely to acquit rather than convict an accused, supporting the balancing role of juries in the face of governmental power.*

Juries have many functions, and the right to a jury trial became a part of our Constitution to balance and check the powers of governmental officials. This was explained in the Supreme Court case of *Duncan v. Louisiana*.

Randolph N. Jonakait, from *The American Jury System*. New Haven, CT: Yale University Press, 2003. Copyright © 2003 by Yale University. All rights reserved. Reproduced by permission.

117

Duncan v. Louisiana:
Checking Abuses of Power

Gary Duncan's criminal trial was seemingly insignificant. He was prosecuted in 1966 in Plaquemines Parish, Louisiana, a strip of land rich in sulphur and oil that stretched a hundred miles from New Orleans down both sides of the Mississippi to the Gulf of Mexico. From the 1920s until his death in 1969, Leander Perez was, according to his biographer Glen Jeansonne, the "political boss who held absolute power in Plaquemines Parish to an extent unsurpassed by any parish leader in Louisiana's history." His base of power for most of this time was as district attorney, an office he passed on in 1960 to his son, Leander Perez, Jr. No one held office and no legislation passed without the father's approval. "Perez, who considered lawmakers superfluous middlemen . . . simply drew up laws and inserted them into the minutes of the parish police jury and commission council. . . . He concluded that honest elections were more trouble than they were worth and made sure none was held in his bailiwick. Dead people might have voted in the elder Richard Daley's Chicago and Lyndon Johnson's Texas, but neither place had Babe Ruth and Charlie Chaplin as voters. Plaquemines did."

Indeed, in 1968 a federal court concluded that the number of white people registered to vote in the parish exceeded the number of white adults who actually lived there. In 1962, although more than a fifth of the sparse population was black, 6,906 white people were registered to vote compared to 43 black people.

On August 26, 1966, the federal courts entered an order desegregating the Plaquemines Parish schools. Leander Perez was not happy. A dozen years earlier, after the Supreme Court had decided *Brown v. Board of Education*, he announced that he was dedicating his life to the principle of segregation. In the 1960s Perez stated, "Do you know what the Negro is? Animals right out of the jungle. Passion. Welfare. Easy life. That's the Negro. And if you don't know that, you're naive." The spearhead for integration came from communistic Zionists, "to all those Jews who were supposed to have been cremated at Buchenwald and Dachau but weren't, and Roosevelt allowed two million of them illegal entry into our country."

The Role of Racism

Gary Duncan's nephew and cousin were two of the black students who began attending a formerly all-white school. On October 18, 1966, they were threatened by white students. The twenty-year-old Duncan, a fisherman, married and with a child, was driving by the school after it let out. He saw a group of white individuals standing near his relatives. He stopped, and his cousin and nephew told him that the white people were trying to start a fight. Duncan herded the two into his car and then "touched" or "slapped" a white boy on the arm. A white adult made a call to the sheriff's office. A deputy spoke to Duncan and the other boys and refused to make an arrest.

Three days later, however, the district attorney, Leander H. Perez, Jr., had Duncan arrested for simple battery because of the touch or slap. Duncan requested a jury trial, but Louisiana then limited jury trials to cases where either capital punishment or imprisonment at hard labor could be imposed. Because simple battery in Louisiana was a misdemeanor carrying a maximum sentence of two years, it did not qualify for a jury trial, and Duncan's trial was held without one. The trial judge convicted the defendant and sentenced Duncan to sixty days in the parish prison plus a $150 fine.

In Plaquemines Parish, Duncan never had a chance of being acquitted. The judge had set bond at twice the usual level. The sentence was longer than for almost any other battery conviction in the parish. Indeed, local lawyers could not be found to defend him. One of his out-of-state lawyers was arrested for illegally practicing law. A federal court eventually enjoined that prosecution, finding that it "was . . . without basis in law and fact." In another decision, a federal court ultimately concluded that Duncan's trial judge had been "personally hostile to Duncan and . . . altered established principles of criminal procedure in an effort to punish Duncan for his exercise of federally secured rights."

Although this was apparently a minor offense, the Supreme Court latched onto the case to make significant constitutional pronouncements. The first concerned the standards for determining whether states have to conform to the provisions in the Bill of Rights of the United States Constitution.

The Bill of Rights and the Fourteenth Amendment

The first ten amendments to the Constitution by their language apply only to the federal government. The Fourteenth Amendment, however, adopted in the wake of the Civil War, denies *states* the power to "deprive any person of life, liberty, or property, without due process of law." The meaning of that phrase is open to various interpretations and over time, the Supreme Court has increasingly looked to the Bill of Rights to define the content of the Fourteenth Amendment's "due process clause."

The Fifth Amendment, for example, requires the federal government to pay just compensation when it takes private property for public purposes. The Fourteenth Amendment does not contain this explicit provision about the public seizure of private property, but before the nineteenth century ended, the Supreme Court held that the Fourteenth Amendment's general due process provision incorporated the Fifth Amendment's more specific command. States, therefore, could constitutionally exercise eminent domain only by giving just compensation even though the Fourteenth Amendment did not specifically enunciate this constitutional principle. Three decades later, the Supreme Court took a similar approach and concluded that the Fourteenth Amendment's general due process clause incorporated the First Amendment's specific provisions concerning speech, press, and religion, and thus, the states could not infringe these rights.

By the 1960s, however, the Supreme Court had still not adopted a similar principle for any of the many Bill of Rights provisions concerning criminal trials. The Court had stated only that the crucial criterion for determining when the states had to confer a criminal procedure safeguard was whether "a civilized system could be imagined that would not accord the particular protection." If the imagination could conjure such a civilized system without the procedure, then the Constitution did not require the states to provide it.

Rejection of the "Imagination" Test

In deciding that states had to afford criminal defendants jury trials, the Court in *Duncan v. Louisiana* rejected this earlier test. The previous standard was wrong, the Court concluded, because state proceedings are not merely abstract schemes, "but actual systems bearing virtually every characteristic of the common-law system that has been developing contemporaneously in England and in this country. The question thus is whether given this kind of system a particular procedure is fundamental—whether, that is, a procedure is necessary to an Anglo-American regime of ordered liberty." The question is not, the Court continued, whether a procedure is "necessarily fundamental to fairness in every criminal system that might be imagined but is fundamental in the context of the criminal processes maintained by the American States."

Under the earlier approach, the Fourteenth Amendment did not require criminal jury trials in state courts. As *Duncan* conceded, a fair criminal process could be imagined that did not utilize juries. Indeed, many civilized countries decide criminal matters without juries. But with the inquiry transformed into whether jury trials are fundamental to the American scheme of criminal justice, the Court concluded that history, modern practices, and the core purposes of juries all indicate that criminal jury trials are so essential that the states are constitutionally required to have them.

Role of Juries in the Colonies

The *Duncan* Court noted that the generation that framed the Constitution viewed jury trials as an essential component of its freedom. Indeed, jury trials came to America with the English colonists, and every colony provided a right to such trials. Moreover, interference with jury trials met with strident protest. The English Stamp Act allowed some violations of revenue laws to be tried in the colonies without juries, but the colonial Stamp Act Congress of 1765 responded that "trial by jury is the inherent and invaluable right of every British subject in these colonies." As England sought to further limit the colonial right to jury trials, the colonists protested more, and the preservation of jury trials became one of the symbols fueling the Revolution. The Declaration of Independence ultimately protested that the king is "depriving us in many cases, of the benefits of Trial by Jury," and to his "transporting us beyond the Seas to be tried for pretended offenses." Not surprisingly, immediately after independence every state guaranteed jury trials. Before the drafting of the federal Constitution, twelve states had adopted their own constitutions. The only right protected in all of them was the right to a jury trial in criminal cases.

The federal Constitution followed suit. The new nation's charter, in article 3, section 2, guaranteed: "The Trial of all Crimes, except in Cases of Impeachment, shall be by Jury; and such Trial shall be held in the State where the said Crimes shall have been committed." Many, however, criticized this Constitution for not adequately protecting criminal jury trials and other rights. The new country soon adopted the first ten amendments, which included another guarantee of jury trials.

The Sixth Amendment states in part: "In all criminal prosecutions, the accused shall enjoy the right to a speedy and public trial, by an impartial jury of the State and district wherein the crime shall have been committed."

Jury trials were fundamentally important at the country's inception. Colonists protested their infringement; all the early states adopted them; the federal Constitution guaranteed criminal jury trials not once, but twice. Furthermore, every state that has since entered the union has protected the right to jury trials in criminal cases. *Duncan v. Louisiana* concluded: "Jury trial continues to receive strong support. The laws of every State guarantee a right to jury trial in serious criminal cases; no State has dispensed with it; nor are there significant movements underway to do so."

More than Just History

The *Duncan* Court built its argument that criminal juries are fundamental to our justice system not merely on historical precedent; it made eloquent reference to the basic legal and societal purposes our juries serve. The widespread use of jury trials reflects "a profound judgment about the way in which law should be enforced and justice administered. A right to jury trial is granted to criminal defendants in order to prevent oppression by the Government." The Court continued that juries can protect society against governmental actors who may use their powers unjustly. "Providing an accused with the right to be tried by a jury of his peers gave him an inestimable safeguard against the corrupt or overzealous prosecutor and against the compliant, biased, or eccentric judge. If the defendant preferred the commonsense judgment of a jury to the more tutored but perhaps less sympathetic reaction of the single judge, he was to have it." Consequently, the Court concluded in *Duncan*, jury trials in criminal cases are fundamental to the American system of justice. The Court held that the Constitution "guarantees a right to jury trial in all criminal cases which—were they to be tried in a federal court—would come within the Sixth Amendment's guarantee."

Some four decades later, many deride juries, but their noise hides the fact that few actually advocate their abolition. Some would like to limit the kinds of civil matters a jury can consider, but no one seriously suggests that juryless tribunals should decide all our criminal cases or even all our civil disputes. There is no movement to repeal the Sixth Amendment's jury trial guarantee. The credible critics are not abolitionists, but reformers. . . .

Checking the Power of Judges

No matter how laws were enacted and no matter how judges obtained and retained office, Americans saw a need to check judicial power. Juries could help do this. As the Supreme Court recognized in *Duncan v. Louisiana*, juries fit into an overall scheme of a government of checks and balances. "[T]he jury trial provisions in the Federal and State Constitutions reflect a fundamental decision about the exercise of official power—a reluctance to entrust plenary powers over the life and liberty of the citizens to one judge or to a group of judges. Fear of unchecked power, so typical of our State and Federal Governments in other respects, found expression in the criminal law in this insistence upon community participation in the determination of guilt or innocence."

Juries are fundamental, according to *Duncan*, not just because of history and not just because they remain in widespread use, but because juries serve crucial societal goals. They prevent governmental oppression by providing a bulwark against unjust laws or unjust prosecutors or unjust judges. But even when laws are fairly enacted, and even when prosecutors and judges are not venal or corrupt, juries are still necessary because the character of human nature indicates that power, especially governmental power, always needs checking. Juries do this. . . .

Juries as a Check on the Corruption of Power

Our government is based on the idea that power, even when exercised by the best, needs to be checked. This view separates the United States from much of the rest of the world and helps explain why we have juries when many places do not. Professor Myron Moskovitz states, "To put it bluntly, Europeans trust authority, and Americans don't. Speaking generally, of course."

The American view is that the need to restrain governmental power may be especially acute in times of crisis, . . . [as at the trial of] Gary Duncan, but the need is ever present because judges, being human, have biases. Thomas Jefferson summarized this need: "We all know that permanent judges acquire an *Esprit de corps*; that being known, they are liable to be tempted by bribery; that they are misled by favor, by relationship, by a spirit of party, by a devotion to the executive or legislative power; that it is better to leave a cause to the decision of cross and pile [i.e., a coin toss], than to that of a judge biased to one side; and that the opinion of twelve honest jurymen gives still a better hope of right, than cross and pile does."

In this Jeffersonian view, all people, not just the venal, become affected by the power they wield. Everyone can be tempted by the forbidden, a point made by the wise old trial judge in James Gould Cozzens's novel *The Just and the Unjust*: "You remember the story of the judge who was offered twenty-five thousand dollars for an opinion favorable to the plaintiff. He threw the man out and when his colleagues sympathized with him over the insult he'd been offered, he said to them: 'Gentlemen, I didn't worry about the insult; you can't insult integrity. What worried me was that he was getting too damned close to my price.'"

Judges can be good people. We can and do have systems to reduce undesirable influences on judges. Nevertheless, the nature of the job affects its holder. Because judges are human, they can be affected by forces that impede neutral decisions and can be tempted by corruption. Juries protect against such human fallibility.

Even Alexander Hamilton, who disagreed with Jefferson over many things, saw juries as a check on judicial corruption. In Number 83 of the *Federalist Papers*, Hamilton stated about trial by jury in civil cases: "The strongest argument in its favor is that it is a security against corruption. As there is always more time and better opportunity to tamper with a standing body of magistrates than with a jury summoned for the occasion, there is room to suppose that a corrupt influence would more easily find its way to the former than to the latter."

Bribing jurors is indeed difficult. Their identity is not known until they are selected at trial. This gives little time to approach them. Perhaps more important, jurors are strangers to the system. Because they come from the community and disappear back into it after the trial, the necessary pathways of solicitation can be hard to discover even if there were time to do so. On the other hand, the identity of the judge is generally known in advance of trial. The judge as a permanent fixture can be studied at some leisure to find approachable avenues. As Hamilton indicated, there will always be more time and opportunity to tamper with permanent judges than with transient jurors.

In addition, the ultimate harm to society is greater when a judge is corrupted than when a jury is compromised. A dishonest juror affects one trial. A crooked judge, however, will hear future cases. Having succumbed once, the odds of yielding again increase. Having acceded, the judge is now vulnerable to blackmail. Thus, the harm of the corrupted judge may continue on beyond one trial.

Juries may diminish the opportunities for bribery and coercion in our trial system, but we cannot know if that is really so. Because we have juries, we cannot know how much judicial corruption there might be without them. Furthermore, when judicial corruption is successful, we do not learn of it, so the extent of the damage is unclear. When such efforts do come to light, however, we tend to hear less about attempts to bribe jurors and more about corrupt judges. "Operation Greylord," for example, led to the conviction of fifteen Chicago judges for bribe-taking and related offenses. Based on what has been revealed historically, at least, we have more to fear from corrupt judges than from corrupt jurors. . . .

Jurors as a Check and Balance in Criminal Cases

In our system, both judges and jury may make factual determinations, but they do not do so for the same issues. Either we have a jury trial or a judge decides; we do not have a hybrid where simultaneously both judge and jury decide the same case. As a consequence, we do not have data about how, if at all, juries and judges differ when deciding the same factual dispute.

The most famous jury study, however, tried to fill this information gap. In the 1950s, Harry Kalven, Jr., and Hans Zeisel surveyed trial judges asking them, among other things, how the jury decided a case and how the judge would have decided it if it had been tried by the judge without a jury. Kalven and Zeisel's groundbreaking book, *The American Jury*, reported that in their sample of 3,576 trials, juries convicted 64.2 percent of the time, acquitted 30.3 percent of the time, and hung 5.5 percent of the time. Judges cannot hang; they have but two choices. The judges in this sample reported that they would have convicted in 83.3 percent of the trials and would have acquitted in 16.7 percent.

The judge concurred with the jury's acquittal in 13.4 percent of the cases and also agreed with 62.05 percent of the convictions. Thus, in three-quarters of the trials, the judge and jury united on the outcome, and if hung juries are counted as half acquittals, then the judge and jury concurred in 78 percent of the cases.

These numbers, however, mask the ways in which judge and jury disagreed. The disagreements, which occurred 22 percent of the time, were strikingly skewed. The jury acquitted 19 percent of the time when the judge would have convicted, and only 3 percent of the time they convicted when the judge would have acquitted. In other words, as Kalven and Zeisel reported, "The jury's disagreement with the judge is massively in one direction, and the direction is the expected one."

As we have seen, juries exist to provide a bulwark against governmental oppression or at least to act as a check on judges who, because of background, training, and position, are likely to side with the government. If the jury is fulfilling its role, then it should be acquitting more often than judges would. Kalven and Zeisel's data indicate that juries are indeed acting as expected—as a check on the judiciary. Or as the Supreme Court in *Duncan v. Louisiana* concluded when it examined these data, "[W]hen juries differ with the result at which the judge would have arrived, it is usually because they are serving some of the very purposes for which they were created and for which they are now employed."

"The circumstances in Duncan *vividly illustrated the civil rights struggle in the Deep South.*"

Duncan v. Louisiana Was a Milestone in the Civil Rights Movement

Nancy J. King

Duncan v. Louisiana *is a case that is intimately entwined with the social upheaval of the late 1960s. In the following article, Vanderbuilt law professor Nancy J. King documents the role of racial tension, crooked politicians, and the entrenched prejudice of the time in the case's facts and its path through the Louisiana state courts to the U.S. Supreme Court. While telling the story of the case, she also documents the effect of the decision on the lives of key players in the drama: defendant Gary Duncan; Judge Leander H. Perez, Sr., the political leader of Plaquemines Parish; and Richard Sobol, the only attorney who was willing to stand up to Perez's grip on the parish and bring Duncan's case the national attention that allowed justice to prevail.*

The criminal jury remains one of the nation's most vital democratic institutions, enabling ordinary citizens to block tyrannical action by government. It is fitting then that the case in which the Court extended the right to a jury trial

Nancy J. King, "The Story of *Duncan v. Louisiana,* 391 U.S. 145 (1968)," *Criminal Procedure Stories,* edited by Carol Steiker. Eagan, MN: Foundation Press, 2006. Copyright © 2006 Thomson West. Reproduced by permission of the publisher and the authors.

to state defendants began in one of the most undemocratic and hierarchical communities in the United States in the 1960s—Plaquemines Parish, Louisiana, 50 miles south of New Orleans.

In 1965, the parish remained in the iron grip of segregationist Judge Leander H. Perez, Sr., a cigar-chomping, thickset, fist-clenching, explosive political leader, with a deep voice and a grey pompadour. Perez had amassed a fortune after welcoming the oil industry to the parish and helping himself to some of the resulting revenues. Serving as District Judge in the parish for five years, then as District Attorney and Parish Council President for nearly fifty years after that, he exercised unquestioned control over all political offices and government services in the parish. He was enormously influential in state politics, saving [Governor] Huey Long from impeachment, and masterminding [Huey's brother] Earl Long into the governor's mansion. The state's "most ardent segregationist," Perez was convinced that Jews were Communists who wanted to conquer America for the Soviet Union by undermining Caucasian stock with miscegenation.

To motivate segregationists, Perez would ask "How would you like it if your little girl came back home ravished from a forced racially integrated school?" "Don't wait for your daughter to be raped by these Congolese," he would exhort his followers. "Don't wait until the burr-heads are forced into your schools. Do something about it now."

Violence followed his speeches. A Catholic school that dared to admit African-American children had its windows shot out and was then bombed. Perez's resistance to integration of Catholic schools led the archbishop of New Orleans to excommunicate him. When court-ordered desegregation came to the state, Perez pushed through the Louisiana legislature a concurrent resolution warning banks and businesses that compliance with the federal court order was illegal and that violators would lose their funds.

Voting rights and other civil liberties in the parish suffered as well. The "Bonaparte of the Bayou" selected the occupant of each post. Elections were a sham. Perez reportedly once said of democracy, "I hate that word." One of his candidates was found to have received 1800 more votes than there were voters registered, causing the unsurprised residents of New Orleans to conclude, "The muskrats must be voting down there." Voters voted in alphabetical order in one election; in another, Babe Ruth, Charlie Chaplin, [and] Herbert Hoover were registered to vote. By August 1965, the United States Attorney General declared Plaquemines Parish one of the nine most discriminatory counties in the nation, with less than 100 of more than 2000 eligible African-American voters registered to vote. After the voting registrar of the parish failed her own voting test, being unable to calculate age based on birth date, and federal investigators arrived, the parish police jury took out an advertisement urging readers not to cooperate with the federal agents. Eventually federal registrars were deployed to the parish, but Perez used them to boost registration of new white voters, outstripping the number of newly registered African-American voters. Perez forbade the local librarian to order books discussing the United Nations, Franklin Delano Roosevelt, or any book "showing a liberal viewpoint," and barred African Americans from checking out books.

He enforced his control over the political, economic, and social life of the parish using first his power as District Attorney, an office he held from 1924 until 1960, when he turned it over to his son, Leander Perez, Jr., then his position as parish Commission Council president from 1961 to 1967 when the presidency passed to his other son, Chalin. Said the elder Perez, "I always take the offensive. The defensive ain't worth a damn." To deter civil rights activists from coming to Plaquemines, Perez converted an abandoned fort in the middle of a swamp into a concentration camp for "racial demonstrators." Accessible only by boat, crawling with snakes, and mosquitoes so thick that cattle couldn't breathe, the fort was given an electrified fence and guard towers by Perez. He gave tours to television crews in which he explained just how he would confine agitators.

By August of 1966, the United States Department of Justice, federal District Judge Christenberry and the Perez establishment were engaged in the opening battles of a vicious desegregation fight. After the school board was notified of the Justice Department's complaint in July, Perez's council order transferred all public school property to the Parish Council. He announced the establishment of a private school for whites. White public school teachers signed contracts with the new private schools after the school board notified them that new contracts with public schools would not be forthcoming. Pianos, audio equipment, maps, aquariums, athletic equipment, textbooks, and new school buses left with the white teachers and students for the new private schools.

By the start of the school year, the five public high schools in the parish had only about half of the students they'd had the year before. At some public schools gyms and auditoriums were reserved for the use of white students from private schools. Public school students had to forego assemblies, organized athletics, and field trips. Damage to the public schools from devastating hurricane Betsy the previous year was ignored, the prices of school lunches tripled, and bookmobiles (the only library service) were rerouted to the new private schools.

Duncan Accused

Bert Grant and Bernard St. Ann, two African-American boys about 12 years old began to attend the formerly all-white Boothville Venice High School that September. They were immediately physically assaulted, threatened, and harassed. On October 18, after being threatened with violence at school again, Bert and Bernard were walking home. Four white boys crossed the road to confront them. Bert and Bernard's cousin, Gary Duncan, age 19, happened to drive by. Duncan, a husband and father, earned about $65 a week as a boat captain. Duncan stopped his car, got out, and asked his cousins what was going on. Bert replied that the white boys wanted to fight, and Duncan told his cousins to get into his car. As they did, Herman Landry, Jr., one of the white boys present, muttered, "You must think you're tough." Duncan then touched Landry on the arm—just how forcefully later became a matter of dispute—urged him to head home, and drove off with Bert and Bernard.

From about 250 feet away, Bert Latham, president of the new private school association established to avoid integration, saw the incident and immediately called the sheriff's office to report that Duncan had slapped Landry Jr.'s arm. A deputy stopped Duncan's car and took him back to the scene. There the deputy questioned the white boys. Landry was not hurt and displayed no bruise. The deputy released Duncan, telling him that he did not believe that he'd struck the boy. Landry Jr.'s father had other ideas. He sought out a justice of the peace and swore out an affidavit supporting Duncan's arrest. On October 21, Gary Duncan was jailed on the charge of cruelty to a juvenile. He was released after his employer posted the $1000 bond.

Gary Duncan and his family doubted that any local attorney would defend him. His concerns were well founded: Leander Perez, Jr., the District Attorney, had stated publicly, "[i]f any known agitator were to appear in Plaquemines Parish, his mere presence would amount to a disturbance of the peace, since he was an outsider." The parish had no African-American attorneys, and African-American lawyers in surrounding areas were reluctant to venture there, after being threatened and compelled to leave in earlier incidents. Some feared that Perez would plant narcotics on them if they went to Plaquemines. One white attorney explaining why he couldn't take a civil rights case said, "These people in town will kill me." Any parish attorney was worthless, Duncan had concluded. As he said later, "all he would have done is get me to plead guilty."

Duncan's parents turned to the Lawyers Constitutional Defense Committee (LCDC), an organization dedicated to litigating civil rights issues in Mississippi, Alabama, and Louisiana. Under the leadership of civil rights attorney Alvin Bronstein and the African-American firm of Niles R. Douglas, Lolis E. Elie, and Robert F. Collins, LCDC had just opened an office in New Orleans. The office and its growing caseload was soon staffed by Richard Sobol, a young white attorney who had moved to New Orleans in August with his wife and two children, taking a leave of absence from Arnold and Porter in Washington, D.C. A meeting was scheduled between Duncan, his witnesses, Sobol, and members of the Douglas, Elie and Collins firm. After the meeting, Sobol and Collins, who later became the Deep South's first African-American United States District Court Judge, took the case. They were already hardpressed to cover dozens of other pending cases needing attention, and knew that the case would involve substantial costs that they would never recover, but they pursued it because "the arrest and prosecution was nothing more than a form of harassment undertaken in retaliation for the fact that Gary Duncan's relatives chose to go to the school previously reserved exclusively for whites."

In State Court

Duncan's trial took place on January 25, 1967. At the state's table sat [assistant district attorney Darryl] Bubrig, accompanied by his boss, Leander Perez, Jr. Sobol appeared for Duncan. He began by filing a jury demand based on the Sixth and Fourteenth Amendments of the United States Constitution. Judge Leon denied the request. In Louisiana, the crime of simple battery was a misdemeanor, punishable at that time by a term of two years' imprisonment and a fine of $300. Crimes not punishable by "imprisonment *[and] hard labor*" were defined under Louisiana law as misdemeanors, and defendants charged with misdemeanors had no right to trial by jury under Louisiana law.

Duncan and his cousins all testified that Duncan had merely touched Landry's elbow, as a manner of expression, while telling him that it would be best if he went home. Latham testified that he saw Duncan slap the white boy in a hostile manner. Although Bubrig conducted the prosecution for the state, during Sobol's attempt to establish acts of violence at school against the two boys, Perez cut in arguing, "[T]hese two colored boys who are witnesses of the defendant had been proven to be the ones who were the aggressors, and I can't understand any further questions along these lines, which to me seemed to tend to prove the guilt of the defendant." Judge Leon too was impatient with this line of testimony, and urged Sobol to stick with "what went on on the side of the road." Ultimately, Judge Leon found the testimony of Latham and Landry more credible than that of the African-American witnesses and convicted Duncan.

At sentencing, Sobol asked for a suspended sentence, but Judge Leon sentenced Duncan to $150, costs, and sixty days in prison, with an additional twenty days if the fine and costs were not paid. This was an extraordinarily stiff sentence for the crime of simple battery. . . .

Sobol then filed notice that he was seeking review in the Louisiana Supreme Court, and after another few hours in jail, Duncan posted an additional $1500 bond imposed by Judge Leon, this time for release pending appeal.

Duncan in his petition for review in the Louisiana Supreme Court argued that the state law permitting trial without jury for a two-year offense violated Duncan's right to a jury trial under the Sixth and Fourteenth Amendments of the United States Constitution. Jury trial, Duncan's attorneys argued, was a fundamental right for those accused of crime, part of the due process guaranteed prior to the deprivation of liberty. The United States Supreme Court had decades earlier rejected this argument; Duncan's attorneys were hoping the [chief justice Earl] Warren Court might see it otherwise. At the time, only two states other than Louisiana denied the right to trial by jury in cases where the defendant faced a sentence of more than six months. The defense argued that "racial overtones were expressed at the trial," and that "in this atmosphere, only a jury composed of a fair representation of the community could impartially assess the evidence and render a just verdict." The petition was summarily denied, due to "no error of law." . . .

In the United States Supreme Court

Sobol's brief in which he was joined by civil rights attorneys Alvin Bronstein, Anthony Amsterdam, and Donald Juneau, argued that Duncan had a right to a jury trial on the battery charge, a right guaranteed by the Fourteenth Amendment's Due Process Clause. Louisiana law denying him a jury trial on the charge carrying up to two years' imprisonment was unconstitutional. Specifically, they asked the Court to overrule its earlier decisions in which it had found that in state court trial by jury, rather than judge, was not required by the Fourteenth Amendment, and that the right to a jury trial in all but petty criminal cases, a right protected by the Sixth Amendment, applied in state prosecutions as well as federal.

The time was right for Duncan's claim. The Warren Court was well underway in what came to be known as the "criminal procedure revolution," in which it expanded the federal judiciary's oversight of state criminal justice by extending to state defendants, one case and constitutional clause at a time, the protections of the Fourth, Fifth, Sixth, and Eighth Amendments previously reserved for federal prosecutions. Over the preceding five terms, the Court had found that due process guaranteed to state as well as federal defendants several other

Sixth Amendment guarantees, including the right to a speedy and public trial, a jury that is impartial, compulsory process, and the right to counsel. Once a right was held to apply to the states, all of the decisions interpreting that right in the federal context were equally applicable to state prosecutions. Through this process of "selective incorporation," the Warren Court had already made it clear that the Constitution regulated the jury process whenever states made it available by barring race discrimination in jury selection, and guaranteeing a jury that was impartial. Duncan's lawyers argued, "It would be ironic indeed if a state were permitted to nullify this Court's carefully developed protections of the jury system by substituting for trial by jury trial by a single judge, who cannot represent a fair cross section of the community and who is frequently exposed to official and unofficial influences prejudicial to the defendant."

Duncan's attorneys argued that the prosecution of their client was just the sort of case where the protection of a jury against the power of judge and prosecutor was most vital, as the prosecution was "part of the general official effort to discourage the exercise of rights under the federal court order" desegregating the local schools. Their argument concluded with a quote from [English jurist William] Blackstone, "In times of difficulty and danger, more is to be apprehended from the violence and partiality of judges appointed by the Crown, in suits between the King and the subject, than in suits between one individual and another. . . ."

On October 9, exactly one week after Judge [Thurgood] Marshall, [the first African-American U.S. Supreme Court Justice] was sworn in as Associate Justice of the United States Supreme Court, the Court noted probable jurisdiction in Duncan's case, and set a date for oral argument. The same day, down in New Orleans, Judge Cassibry granted a motion to allow Arnold and Porter to participate as amici [friends of the court] in Sobol's lawsuit. Ultimately Sobol's cause was joined by the United States Department of Justice, the NAACP [National Association for the Advancement of Colored People], and thirty of the nation's leading law firms.

None of this seemed to faze the Perez establishment in the least. Attorneys in the Perez camp, while simultaneously resisting Duncan's appeal . . . and sabotaging the federal efforts to end segregation and African-American disenfranchisement in the parish, continued to deal with political enemies by locking them up. That December, one foe who was alleged to have threatened Judge Perez was forced to post over $31,000 in bonds in order to gain his freedom. And in an ironic twist, while Duncan's case was winding its way through its appellate stages, parish officials defending against the Justice Department's school desegregation suit protested that they were "entitled to the right of trial by jury," in the case "because the government's suit against it was in the nature of a suit to try the title to land," a claim summarily rejected by the federal court.

Duncan's attorneys argued to the Court that extending the right of jury trial to the states was imperative in order to end racial injustice in the Deep South. Factual findings by judges, in particular, credibility determinations like the ones Judge Leon had made in Duncan's case, were virtually unreviewable.

> [I]n cases such as this—where the personal and political leanings of the trial judge will often be antagonistic to the defendant—the potential for a factual determination that is influenced by considerations other than the evidence of record is very great. This situation, particularly in civil rights related prosecutions in the Deep South, is not uncommon. Because of the accepted limitation on federal review and state appellate review of factual determinations in state trial courts, the only effective remedy is to guarantee the accused the right to have the crucial factual determination of guilt or innocence made by a jury, rather than by a judge. . . .

To this instrumentalist justification, they added historical practice, as well as the weight of authority in other states, arguing that the right to a jury trial in non-petty offenses was fundamental, so fundamental that it was part of the due process guaranteed by the Fourteenth Amendment.

Louisiana Attorney General Jack Gremillion selected attorney Dorothy Wolbrette to brief and argue Duncan's case for the state. One of only three women in her graduating class, Wolbrette had been editor-in-chief of the *Tulane Law Review* in 1944–45, and had practiced law with her father prior to landing a job with the state. Wolbrette remembered, "All these liberal groups had sent us this big, thick brief that they researched for ages and had been waiting to use." The *Duncan* case, she later said, was about the political and social sensibilities of the 1960s. Gremillion would later recall, "I was at the helm of the state's legal team during all the cases when Louisiana lost its sovereignty to the federal government."

Louisiana argued to the Court that history did not support treating the right to a jury trial as a fundamental right, that a fair trial did not depend upon the presence of a jury, and even if the Sixth Amendment did guarantee a right to trial by jury, surely it wouldn't extend to a case in which the defendant was charged with an offense classified as a misdemeanor under state law and treated as a petty offense in almost every jurisdiction, for which the defendant received only 60 days' imprisonment. Any jury required by due process, the state argued, need not mirror exactly the Sixth Amendment jury that federal defendants enjoyed—a twelve-person, unanimous jury for any offense carrying a penalty of over six months' imprisonment.

This plea for less than wholesale application of all aspects of an individual right to the states had a basis in some prior opinions of the justices. But adherents for incomplete application were dwindling. Repeatedly in earlier cases, the Court had required states to comply with all features of what formerly had been strictly federal rights. Only a minority of the justices had expressed opposition to applying all specific aspects of each right against the states. These justices preferred instead to require only those processes that were required by "fundamental fairness."

Justice Byron White drafted the majority opinion reversing the Louisiana Supreme Court's rejection of the right to jury. . . .

Aftermath

Despite the important victories of . . . *Duncan*, it was business as usual in Plaquemines Parish for some time. One determined Perez opponent, Lawrence Rousselle, was arrested by Lea Perez, Jr., for plotting to assassinate Judge Perez. Rousselle had dared to encourage whites to attend integrated schools and support a candidate challenging Chalin Perez for council president. Held for two weeks on a $75,000 bond (later reduced by the Supreme Court of Louisiana), he was finally released after Chalin Perez won the election, with no indictment or information ever filed. Prosecuted again the next year, Rousselle filed false imprisonment claims and dashed off to federal court in New Orleans to seek removal of the state criminal charges to federal court.

The day Judge Perez died in 1969, five young African-American men entered a parish bar and "rashly announced their intention to celebrate." The five were quickly arrested, charged, and convicted of drunkenness and disturbing the peace (neither offense triggering the right to trial by jury under *Duncan*) and sentenced to jail with no option of paying a fine. One wonders whether bar patrons celebrating something else would have paid as high a price.

Voting rights efforts in the parish had actually lost ground. As of 1970 only 184 out of nearly 3000 African-American residents eligible to vote were registered. Plaqueminians did not have their first free election until the early 1980s, when

Judge Perez's two sons turned against each other, creating an opening for opposition forces. Lea, Jr., started investigating the council in the late 1970s, and the grand jury indicted his brother Chalin in 1981. But in 1982, the grand jury indicted Lea Perez, Jr., and Judge Leon with conspiracy and malfeasance involving their role in the early discharge of a 1981 grand jury that was allegedly planning to indict Perez, Jr. By 1983, Chalin Perez had been ousted from the council presidency. Lea Perez, Jr., chose not run for re-election as District Attorney. A suit against the Perez family by the Parish government seeking millions in oil royalties accumulated unlawfully between 1936 and 1983 was settled in 1987 for $12 million and future oil earnings. Darryl Bubrig, the Assistant District Attorney who had tried the battery charge against Duncan to Judge Leon, took the reins from Leander Perez, Jr., in 1984 and is still today the Plaquemines District Attorney.

Duncan later bought a shrimp boat, and when it was destroyed by a collision with an underwater oil jacket, he hired Sobol to represent him in a successful suit against the oil company. Still piloting boats in the parish today, Duncan was selected to receive a local 2003 Black History Month Award. . . .

Conclusion

Like the facts of so many other criminal cases reviewed by the Court during the 1950s and 60s, the circumstances in *Duncan* vividly illustrated the civil rights struggle in the Deep South. The conflict between parish officials and Gary Duncan grew out of the violent response of white citizens to school desegregation, and grew into a fight for the rights of minority citizens to secure legal counsel of their choice. The decision also became the focus of one of the most fundamental controversies in constitutional law, a case in which the justices openly debated federal regulation of state government. The Court's selective incorporation approach in *Duncan*, hardly controversial now, was an explosive state's rights issue at the time. As

Justice [William] Brennan later wrote, it was in *Duncan* that the Court "attempted to explain the theoretical basis for its decisions requiring the states to adhere to certain provisions of the Bill [of Rights] while excluding others."

That the right to trial by jury became the vehicle for resolving such a vital constitutional question is not surprising. Of all of the rights of those accused of crime, it is the only right that is enshrined in all of the original state constitutions, and in the body of the United States Constitution itself. Not even the right to counsel shares this distinction. The jury is more than a safeguard against inaccuracy or prosecutorial overreaching; it is a unique political force. Ordinary jurors can thwart the power of the judiciary in ways that procedures guaranteed by other rights of those accused of crime cannot. Federal judicial oversight of state criminal prosecutions threaten state autonomy from without, but jury rights, like voting rights, threaten state power from within. *Duncan*'s holding that the Due Process Clause limits a state's power to deny jury trials was a key element of the Warren Court's expansive efforts to ensure that the criminal processes of state government would not be used as a weapon against those struggling to assert their civil rights.

"The Justices ruled that virtually any question that could boost someone's maximum sentence . . . must be decided by a trial jury."

Duncan's Expansion of the Right to a Jury Trial Also Expanded the Role of Juries in Sentencing Criminal Defendants

Laurie Asseo

The groundbreaking Supreme Court holding in Duncan v. Louisiana *left open many important questions about the use of jury trials in criminal prosecutions. Among these questions was the role of the jury in sentencing decisions. Traditionally, after the guilt of an accused person was determined, the jury was excused and the judge went on to determine the appropriate sentence for the crime. It was accepted that the judge took into account actions of the defendant that may not have been told the jury or proven beyond a reasonable doubt. This traditional approach was challenged and overturned in June 2000 with* Apprendi v. New Jersey, *which held that under the Sixth Amendment of the Constitution, sentencing was an appropriate issue for the jury to consider. In the following article, reporter Laurie Asseo discusses the rise in criminal appeals seeking shorter sentences that has resulted from this decision.*

Laurie Asseo, "Expanded Right to Jury Trial Means More Appeals for Criminal Defendants," *The Post*, October 30, 2000. Reprinted with permission of the Associated Press.

The Supreme Court is seeing the effects of . . . [the] ground-breaking ruling which expands jury-trial rights in certain criminal cases: A pile of appeals by defendants who say their sentences are unfair.

The Justices ruled that virtually any question that could boost someone's maximum sentence, such as whether a crime was motivated by racial hate, must be decided by a trial jury. Judges no longer can decide such issues on their own during sentencing.

In essence, the Court said the constitutional right to trial by jury means what it says, said New York lawyer Gerald Lefcourt, former president of the National Association of Criminal Defense Lawyers. That's been bedrock U.S. justice since the Founding Fathers.

There are dozens of cases that have come down the pike already challenging sentences as a result of the ruling, said Miami criminal defense lawyer Neal Sonnett. However, he added, whether it has far-reaching effects is yet to be determined.

The ruling [*Apprendi v. New Jersey*, 530 U.S. 466 (2000)] . . . said a New Jersey man who fired shots into a black family's home was entitled to have a jury decide whether he acted out of hate and could be sent to prison longer than the ordinary maximum.

New appeals citing that decision are rolling in to the Supreme Court, and the Justices already have ordered lower courts to take a new look at a number of cases. Lower courts have decided some defendants are entitled to a new sentencing.

Many of those cases involve drugs. Until now, judges often have decided such issues as how much cocaine someone sold: more cocaine can lead to a longer prison sentence. But many appeals say those decisions now must be made by the jury if the drug quantity could boost the maximum sentence.

Other appeals say juries must decide such issues as the amount of loss in a fraud case, or a defendant's use of a gun, if that factor would allow a longer maximum prison term.

Prosecutors also are figuring out how to comply with the ruling in future cases.

Justice Department officials say the ruling will require prosecutors to prove more facts to juries when those facts would allow a longer maximum sentence.

Monmouth County, N.J., prosecutor John Kaye said many state laws allow higher maximum sentences if prosecutors show, for example, that someone is a career criminal, is involved with a street gang or committed a crime by using a stolen car.

All those things will be tested now, Kaye said, adding that proving such issues to a jury instead of a judge would be a little harder, but we'll work with it.

The whole issue stems from the Constitution's Sixth Amendment guarantee of a jury trial for criminal defendants. Even with that guarantee, trial judges traditionally have had wide leeway to impose sentences by considering all of a defendant's actions, even if they were not charged or proved to the jury.

CHAPTER 4

The Right to Confront One's Accusers

Chapter Preface

Case Overview: The Supreme Court decision in the case of *Crawford v. Washington* (2004) examined whether the taped testimony of Sylvia Crawford (without her courtroom appearance) in the trial of her husband, Michael Crawford, amounted to a violation of his constitutional right to confront his accusers under the Sixth Amendment. He had been accused of the assault and attempted murder of another man, Kenneth Lee, in the presence of Sylvia Crawford. Michael Crawford claimed his actions were in self-defense. The statement of his wife contradicted his, and he invoked marital privilege to stop her from testifying against him. Sylvia Crawford did not appear in the courtroom, but the state introduced her taped, contradictory statement, and Michael Crawford was convicted.

Crawford appealed his guilty verdict to the Washington Court of Appeals, and then to the Washington Supreme Court, on the grounds that his Sixth Amendment right to confront his accuser (his wife was called a nontestifying accomplice) was violated. The Court of Appeals reversed his conviction, finding Sylvia's statements were so unreliable that introducing them only on tape was unconstitutional. The Supreme Court of Washington returned to the original trial court position and reinstated the conviction, finding the disagreement of the two statements was minor enough to make Sylvia's testimony reliable, and thus constitutionally admissible.

Crawford then took his cause to the U.S. Supreme Court, which accepted it for review. The justices agreed with his arguments; Justice Antonin Scalia wrote the majority opinion of the Court, which overruled the "reliability" test that had been used by the Washington state courts to get such differing results. Instead, he proposed a new "bright line" test (i.e., one less vague) that stated that if the evidence is testimonial, the witness is unavailable, and there has been no opportunity for cross-examination, entry of this testimony in a criminal case is unconstitutional, as it violates the Sixth Amendment right of an accused to confront his or her accusers.

Scalia began the opinion with a review of the history of the Confrontation Clause in English and American courts. He described one particular case as the evil the Confrontation Clause was intended to address, the use of testimony by absent witnesses in the treason trial of Sir Walter Raleigh. He also reviewed the central role of the need for cross-examination in the history of this right. Scalia went on to strongly criticize the so-called reliability test, stating that not only were the results inconsistent, the test erred by letting testimony stand that historically would have been excluded. Thus, the new test requiring testimony in court with the opportunity to cross-examine had to be applied to set the record straight.

Chief Justice William H. Rehnquist authored the concurring opinion in *Crawford*. In Rehnquist's view, the existing reliability test was sufficient to reverse Crawford's conviction, and no new test need be formulated for this case. He expressed concern about the effect the new test would have on criminal prosecutions around the nation and the need for stability when it comes to such determinations. Rehnquist did not believe that the majority's historical analysis of what the Sixth Amendment would or would not have protected at the time of the drafting of the Constitution was sufficiently persuasive to require the new test.

The impact of *Crawford* has focused on a particular subset of criminal cases: sexual assault cases in which the victim or witness is unable to testify in court and domestic violence cases where the victim refuses to testify against the accused batterer. It has also opened a new analysis of the various statements that are offered as evidence in court—whether or not these statements can be seen as "testimonial" and thus falling within the protective guidelines set forth in *Crawford*. If the statements are *not* testimony, they are admissible even without the witness present or the use of cross-examination.

A particular example of "nontestimony" used by the prosecution to avoid the *Crawford* test is a claim that the contested statement, when made outside of court under high emotional stress, should be classified as "an excited utterance." This is a common occurrence for statements at issue in sexual assault and domestic violence cases. Since the statement was made outside of court, it is considered hearsay and generally barred from admission. But on the theory that the emotion behind the statement makes it more truthful, excited utterances are considered exceptions to the hearsay rule and are admitted as "nontestimonial" evidence under *Crawford*. In 2006 the Supreme Court agreed to review two cases, *Davis v. Washington* and *Hammon v. Indiana*, which address whether courts are correctly applying this "excited utterance" exception or unacceptably expanding the hearsay exception to avoid the guidelines of *Crawford*. Ultimately, only over time will the full impact of this decision on criminal prosecutions be understood.

> "Where testimonial evidence is at issue
> ... the Sixth Amendment demands
> what the common law required: un-
> availability and a prior opportunity for
> cross-examination."

The Court's Majority Opinion: The Constitutional Right to Confront One's Accusers Needs a New Test for the Admissibility of Evidence

Antonin Scalia

*In 1999 Washington State resident Michael Crawford was ac-
cused and convicted of the assault and attempted murder of a
man who allegedly was sexually assaulting Crawford's wife,
Sylvia. Crawford claimed self-defense. At the trial, however, the
state introduced a recorded statement his wife had made while
under police interrogation that contradicted a self-defense sce-
nario. Sylvia did not testify in court because her husband had
invoked marital privilege, under which one's spouse cannot be
compelled to testify against one. Crawford appealed his conviction on the grounds that Sylvia's taped testimony violated his
right to confront his accusers, as guaranteed by the Sixth
Amendment's so-called Confrontation Clause. Because Sylvia
was an unavailable witness, and Crawford's attorney was denied
the opportunity to ask questions—that is, to cross-examine her—
the Supreme Court ruled in Crawford's favor. Justice Antonin
Scalia wrote the majority opinion, in which he also formulated a*

Antonin Scalia, majority opinion, *Crawford v. Washington*, 541 US 36 (2004).

new test for the admissibility of evidence from an unavailable witness. Scalia has served on the Supreme Court since 1986.

The Sixth Amendment's Confrontation Clause provides that, "[i]n all criminal prosecutions, the accused shall enjoy the right ... to be confronted with the witnesses against him." We have held that this bedrock procedural guarantee applies to both federal and state prosecutions.... [*Ohio v.*] *Roberts* says that an unavailable witness's out-of-court statement may be admitted so long as it has adequate indicia of reliability—*i.e.*, falls within a "firmly rooted hearsay exception" or bears "particularized guarantees of trustworthiness." Petitioner argues that this test strays from the original meaning of the Confrontation Clause and urges us to reconsider it.

History of the Confrontation Clause

The Constitution's text does not alone resolve this case. One could plausibly read "witnesses against" a defendant to mean those who actually testify at trial, those whose statements are offered at trial, or something in-between. We must therefore turn to the historical background of the Clause to understand its meaning.

The right to confront one's accusers is a concept that dates back to Roman times. The founding generation's immediate source of the concept, however, was the common law. English common law has long differed from continental civil law in regard to the manner in which witnesses give testimony in criminal trials. The common-law tradition is one of live testimony in court subject to adversarial testing, while the civil law condones examination in private by judicial officers.

Nonetheless, England at times adopted elements of the civil-law practice. Justices of the peace or other officials examined suspects and witnesses before trial. These examinations were sometimes read in court in lieu of live testimony, a practice that "occasioned frequent demands by the prisoner to have his 'accusers,' *i.e.* the witnesses against him, brought before him face to face." . . .

Many declarations of rights adopted around the time of the Revolution guaranteed a right of confrontation. . . . The proposed Federal Constitution, however, did not. At the Massachusetts ratifying convention, Abraham Holmes objected to this omission precisely on the ground that it would lead to civil-law practices: "The mode of trial is altogether indetermined; . . . whether [the defendant] is to be allowed to confront the witnesses, and have the advantage of cross-examination, we are not yet told. . . . [W]e shall find Congress possessed of powers enabling them to institute judicatories little less inauspicious than a certain tribunal in Spain, . . . [that is,] the *Inquisition*." . . . The First Congress responded by including the Confrontation Clause in the proposal that became the Sixth Amendment. . . .

The Example of Sir Walter Raleigh

The most notorious instances of civil-law examination occurred in the great political trials of the 16th and 17th centuries. One such was the 1603 trial of Sir Walter Raleigh for treason. Lord Cobham, Raleigh's alleged accomplice, had implicated him in an examination before the Privy Council and in a letter. At Raleigh's trial, these were read to the jury. Raleigh argued that Cobham had lied to save himself. "Cobham is absolutely in the King's mercy; to excuse me cannot avail him; by accusing me he may hope for favour." Suspecting that Cobham would recant, Raleigh demanded that the judges call him to appear, arguing that "[t]he Proof of the Common Law is by witness and jury: let Cobham be here, let him speak it. Call my accuser before my face. . . ." The judges refused, and, despite Raleigh's protestations that he was being tried "by the Spanish Inquisition," the jury convicted, and Raleigh was sentenced to death.

One of Raleigh's trial judges later lamented that "'the justice of England has never been so degraded and injured as by the condemnation of Sir Walter Raleigh.'" Through a series of statutory and judicial reforms, English law developed a right of confrontation that limited these abuses. For example, treason statutes required witnesses to confront the accused "face to face" at his arraignment. Courts, meanwhile, developed relatively strict rules of unavailability, admitting examinations only if the witness was demonstrably unable to testify in person. Several authorities also stated that a suspect's confession could be admitted only against himself, and not against others he implicated. . . .

One recurring question was whether the admissibility of an unavailable witness's pretrial examination depended on whether the defendant had had an opportunity to cross-examine him. In 1696, the Court of King's Bench answered this question in the affirmative, in the widely reported misdemeanor libel case of *King* v. *Paine*, 5 Mod. 163, 87 Eng. Rep. 584. The court ruled that, even though a witness was dead, his examination was not admissible where "the defendant not being present when [it was] taken before the mayor . . . had lost the benefit of a cross-examination." . . .

Absent Witnesses Decried

This history supports two inferences about the meaning of the Sixth Amendment.

First, the principal evil at which the Confrontation Clause was directed was the civil-law mode of criminal procedure, and particularly its use of *ex parte* examinations as evidence against the accused. It was these practices that the Crown deployed in notorious treason cases like Raleigh's; . . . , that English law's assertion of a right to confrontation was meant to prohibit; and that the founding-era rhetoric decried. The Sixth Amendment must be interpreted with this focus in mind.

Accordingly, we once again reject the view that the Confrontation Clause applies of its own force only to in-court testimony, and that its application to out-of-court statements introduced at trial depends upon "the law of Evidence for the time being." Leaving the regulation of out-of-court statements to the law of evidence would render the Confrontation Clause powerless to prevent even the most flagrant inquisitorial practices. Raleigh was, after all, perfectly free to confront those who read Cobham's confession in court.

This focus also suggests that not all hearsay implicates the Sixth Amendment's core concerns. An off-hand, overheard remark might be unreliable evidence and thus a good candidate for exclusion under hearsay rules, but it bears little resemblance to the civil-law abuses the Confrontation Clause targeted. On the other hand, *ex parte* examinations might sometimes be admissible under modern hearsay rules, but the Framers [of the U.S. Constitution] certainly would not have condoned them. . . .

The Need for Cross-Examination

The historical record also supports a second proposition: that the Framers would not have allowed admission of testimonial statements of a witness who did not appear at trial unless he was unavailable to testify, and the defendant had had a prior opportunity for cross-examination. The text of the Sixth Amendment does not suggest any open-ended exceptions from the confrontation requirement to be developed by the courts. Rather, the "right . . . to be confronted with the witnesses against him," Amdt. 6, is most naturally read as a reference to the right of confrontation at common law, admitting only those exceptions established at the time of the founding. As the English authorities above reveal, the common law in 1791 conditioned admissibility of an absent witness's examination on unavailability and a prior opportunity to cross-examine. The Sixth Amendment therefore incorporates those limitations. . . .

Our case law has been largely consistent with these two principles. Our leading early decision, for example, involved a deceased witness's prior trial testimony. *Mattox* v. *United States*, 156 U.S. 237 (1895). In allowing the statement to be admitted, we relied on the fact that the defendant had had, at the first trial, an adequate opportunity to confront the witness: "The substance of the constitutional protection is preserved to the prisoner in the advantage he has once had of seeing the witness face to face, and of subjecting him to the ordeal of a cross-examination. This, the law says, he shall under no circumstances be deprived of. . . ."

Our cases have thus remained faithful to the Framers' understanding: Testimonial statements of witnesses absent from trial have been admitted only where the declarant is unavailable, and only where the defendant has had a prior opportunity to cross-examine.

Problems with "Reliability" Test

Although the results of our decisions have generally been faithful to the original meaning of the Confrontation Clause, the same cannot be said of our rationales. *Roberts* conditions the admissibility of all hearsay evidence on whether it falls under a "firmly rooted hearsay exception" or bears "particularized guarantees of trustworthiness." 448 U. S., at 66. This test departs from the historical principles identified above in two respects. First, it is too broad: It applies the same mode of analysis whether or not the hearsay consists of *ex parte* testimony. This often results in close constitutional scrutiny in cases that are far removed from the core concerns of the Clause. At the same time, however, the test is too narrow: It admits statements that *do* consist of *ex parte* testimony upon a mere finding of reliability. This malleable standard often fails to protect against paradigmatic confrontation violations. . . .

Where testimonial statements are involved, we do not think the Framers meant to leave the Sixth Amendment's protection to the vagaries of the rules of evidence, much less to amorphous notions of "reliability." Certainly none of the authorities discussed above acknowledges any general reliability exception to the common-law rule. Admitting statements deemed reliable by a judge is fundamentally at odds with the right of confrontation. To be sure, the Clause's ultimate goal is to ensure reliability of evidence, but it is a procedural rather than a substantive guarantee. It commands, not that evidence be reliable, but that reliability be assessed in a particular manner: by testing in the crucible of cross-examination. The Clause thus reflects a judgment, not only about the desirability of reliable evidence (a point on which there could be little dissent), but about how reliability can best be determined.

The *Roberts* test allows a jury to hear evidence, untested by the adversary process, based on a mere judicial determination of reliability. It thus replaces the constitutionally prescribed method of assessing reliability with a wholly foreign one. In this respect, it is very different from exceptions to the Confrontation Clause that make no claim to be a surrogate means of assessing reliability. For example, the rule of forfeiture by wrongdoing (which we accept) extinguishes confrontation claims on essentially equitable grounds; it does not purport to be an alternative means of determining reliability.

The Raleigh trial itself involved the very sorts of reliability determinations that *Roberts* authorizes. In the face of Raleigh's repeated demands for confrontation, the prosecution responded with many of the arguments a court applying *Roberts* might invoke today: that Cobham's statements were self-inculpatory, that they were not made in the heat of passion, and that they were not "extracted from [him] upon any hopes or promise of Pardon." It is not plausible that the Framers' only objection to the trial was that Raleigh's judges did not properly weigh these factors before sentencing him to death. Rather, the problem was that the judges refused to allow Raleigh to confront Cobham in court, where he could cross-examine him and try to expose his accusal as a lie.

Dispensing with confrontation because testimony is obviously reliable is akin to dispensing with jury trial because a defendant is obviously guilty. This is not what the Sixth Amendment prescribes.

The legacy of *Roberts* in other courts vindicates the Framers' wisdom in rejecting a general reliability exception. The framework is so unpredictable that it fails to provide meaningful protection from even core confrontation violations.

Reliability is an amorphous, if not entirely subjective, concept. There are countless factors bearing on whether a statement is reliable. . . . Whether a statement is deemed reliable depends heavily on which factors the judge considers and how much weight he accords each of them. . . .

The unpardonable vice of the *Roberts* test, however, is not its unpredictability, but its demonstrated capacity to admit core testimonial statements that the Confrontation Clause plainly meant to exclude. . . . One recent study found that . . . appellate courts admitted accomplice statements to the authorities in 25 out of 70 cases—more than one-third of the time. Courts have invoked *Roberts* to admit other sorts of plainly testimonial statements despite the absence of any opportunity to cross-examine. . . .

That inculpating statements are given in a testimonial setting is not an antidote to the confrontation problem, but rather the trigger that makes the Clause's demands most urgent. It is not enough to point out that most of the usual safeguards of the adversary process attend the statement, when the single safeguard missing is the one the Confrontation Clause demands.

Applying *Roberts* to the Present Facts

Roberts' failings were on full display in the proceedings below. Sylvia Crawford made her statement while in police custody, herself a potential suspect in the case. Indeed, she had been told that whether she would be released "depend[ed] on how the investigation continues." In response to often leading questions from police detectives, she implicated her husband in Lee's stabbing and at least arguably undermined his self-defense claim. Despite all this, the trial court admitted her statement, listing several reasons why it was reliable. In its opinion reversing, the Court of Appeals listed several *other* reasons why the statement was *not* reliable. Finally, the State Supreme Court relied exclusively on the interlocking character of the statement and disregarded every other factor the lower courts had considered. The case is thus a self-contained demonstration of *Roberts*' unpredictable and inconsistent application.

Each of the courts also made assumptions that cross-examination might well have undermined. The trial court, for example, stated that Sylvia Crawford's statement was reliable because she was an eyewitness with direct knowledge of the events. But Sylvia at one point told the police that she had "shut [her] eyes and . . . didn't really watch" part of the fight, and that she was "in shock." The trial court also buttressed its reliability finding by claiming that Sylvia was "being questioned by law enforcement, and, thus, the [questioner] is . . . neutral to her and not someone who would be inclined to advance her interests and shade her version of the truth unfavorably toward the defendant." The Framers would be astounded to learn that *ex parte* testimony could be admitted against a criminal defendant because it was elicited by "neutral" government officers. But even if the court's assessment of the officer's motives was accurate, it says nothing about Sylvia's perception of her situation. Only cross-examination could reveal that.

The State Supreme Court gave dispositive weight to the interlocking nature of the two statements—that they were both ambiguous as to when and whether Lee had a weapon.

The court's claim that the two statements were *equally* ambiguous is hard to accept. Petitioner's statement is ambiguous only in the sense that he had lingering doubts about his recollection: "I coulda swore I seen him goin' for somethin' before, right before everything happened. . . . [B]ut I'm not positive." Sylvia's statement, on the other hand, is truly inscrutable, since the key timing detail was simply assumed in the leading question she was asked: "Did Kenny do anything to fight back from this assault?" Moreover, Sylvia specifically said Lee had nothing in his hands after he was stabbed, while petitioner was not asked about that.

The prosecutor obviously did not share the court's view that Sylvia's statement was ambiguous—he called it "damning evidence" that "completely refutes [petitioner's] claim of self-defense." We have no way of knowing whether the jury agreed with the prosecutor or the court. Far from obviating the need for cross-examination, the "interlocking" ambiguity of the two statements made it all the more imperative that they be tested to tease out the truth.

We readily concede that we could resolve this case by simply reweighing the "reliability factors" under *Roberts* and finding that Sylvia Crawford's statement falls short. But we view this as one of those rare cases in which the result below is so improbable that it reveals a fundamental failure on our part to interpret the Constitution in a way that secures its intended constraint on judicial discretion. Moreover, to reverse the Washington Supreme Court's decision after conducting our own reliability analysis would perpetuate, not avoid, what the Sixth Amendment condemns. The Constitution prescribes a procedure for determining the reliability of testimony in criminal trials, and we, no less than the state courts, lack authority to replace it with one of our own devising.

We have no doubt that the courts below were acting in utmost good faith when they found reliability. The Framers, however, would not have been content to indulge this assumption. They knew that judges, like other government officers, could not always be trusted to safeguard the rights of the people. . . . They were loath to leave too much discretion in judicial hands. By replacing categorical constitutional guarantees with open-ended balancing tests, we do violence to their design. Vague standards are manipulable, and, while that might be a small concern in run-of-the-mill assault prosecutions like this one, the Framers had an eye toward politically charged cases like Raleigh's—great state trials where the impartiality of even those at the highest levels of the judiciary might not be so clear. It is difficult to imagine *Roberts* providing any meaningful protection in those circumstances.

Availability and Cross-Examination Required

Where nontestimonial hearsay is at issue, it is wholly consistent with the Framers' design to afford the States flexibility in their development of hearsay law—as does *Roberts*, and as would an approach that exempted such statements from Confrontation Clause scrutiny altogether. Where testimonial evidence is at issue, however, the Sixth Amendment demands what the common law required: unavailability and a prior opportunity for cross-examination. We leave for another day any effort to spell out a comprehensive definition of "testimonial." Whatever else the term covers, it applies at a minimum to prior testimony at a preliminary hearing, before a grand jury, or at a former trial; and to police interrogations. These are the modern practices with closest kinship to the abuses at which the Confrontation Clause was directed.

In this case, the State admitted Sylvia's testimonial statement against petitioner, despite the fact that he had no opportunity to cross-examine her. That alone is sufficient to make out a violation of the Sixth Amendment. *Roberts* notwithstanding, we decline to mine the record in search of indicia of reliability. Where testimonial statements are at issue, the only indicium of reliability sufficient to satisfy constitutional demands is the one the Constitution actually prescribes: confrontation.

The judgment of the Washington Supreme Court is reversed, and the case is remanded for further proceedings not inconsistent with this opinion.

It is so ordered.

> "I believe that the Court's adoption of a new interpretation of the Confrontation Clause is not backed by sufficiently persuasive reasoning to overrule long-established precedent."

The Court's Concurring Opinion: The Constitutional Right to Confront One's Accusers Is Protected by the Old Reliability Test for the Admissibility of Evidence

William H. Rehnquist

Supreme Court chief justice William H. Rehnquist agreed with the majority opinion in Crawford v. Washington *that Sylvia Crawford's testimony against her husband should not be allowed to stand, and Crawford's conviction should be overturned because his constitutional right to confront his accusers under the Sixth Amendment were violated. Rehnquist disagreed, however, with the majority opinion that the "reliability" test set forth in* Ohio v. Roberts *needed a new interpretation. The reliability test states that the fact that a witness is unable to testify in court does not preclude testimony's admissibility as evidence if the testimony has guarantees of trustworthiness or reliability.*

Rehnquist asserted that Sylvia's statement was sufficiently unreliable to satisfy the Roberts *test. Thus, Rehnquist urged that unreliability be used to find the entry of the testimony unconstitutional. Then the new test put forth by Justice Antonin Scalia,*

William H. Rehnquist, concurring opinion, *Crawford v. Washington*, 541 US 36 (2004).

and the uncertainty that new legal tests bring to criminal proceedings, would be unnecessary. Rehnquist died in September 2005 at the age of eighty, having served on the Court for thirty-three years.

I dissent from the Court's decision to overrule *Ohio* v. *Roberts*, 448 U. S. 56 (1980). I believe that the Court's adoption of a new interpretation of the Confrontation Clause is not backed by sufficiently persuasive reasoning to overrule long-established precedent. Its decision casts a mantle of uncertainty over future criminal trials in both federal and state courts, and is by no means necessary to decide the present case.

Testimonial vs. Nontestimonial Statements

The Court's distinction between testimonial and nontestimonial statements, contrary to its claim, is no better rooted in history than our current doctrine. Under the common law, although the courts were far from consistent, out-of-court statements made by someone other than the accused and not taken under oath, unlike *ex parte* depositions or affidavits, were generally not considered substantive evidence upon which a conviction could be based. Testimonial statements such as accusatory statements to police officers likely would have been disapproved of in the 18th century, not necessarily because they resembled *ex parte* affidavits or depositions, as the Court reasons, but more likely than not because they were not made under oath. Without an oath, one usually did not get to the second step of whether confrontation was required.

Thus, while I agree that the Framers were mainly concerned about sworn affidavits and depositions, it does not follow that they were similarly concerned about the Court's broader category of testimonial statements. As far as I can tell, unsworn testimonial statements were treated no differently at common law than were nontestimonial statements, and it seems to me any classification of statements as testimonial beyond that of sworn affidavits and depositions will be somewhat arbitrary, merely a proxy for what the Framers might have intended had such evidence been liberally admitted as substantive evidence like it is today.

I therefore see no reason why the distinction the Court draws is preferable to our precedent. We have never drawn a distinction between testimonial and nontestimonial statements. And for that matter, neither has any other court of which I am aware. I see little value in trading our precedent for an imprecise approximation at this late date.

I am also not convinced that the Confrontation Clause categorically requires the exclusion of testimonial statements. Although many States had their own Confrontation Clauses, they were of recent vintage and were not interpreted with any regularity before 1791. State cases that recently followed the ratification of the Sixth Amendment were not uniform; the Court itself cites state cases from the early 19th century that took a more stringent view of the right to confrontation than does the Court, prohibiting former testimony even if the witness was subjected to cross-examination. . . .

Exceptions Do Not Denigrate

To find exceptions to exclusion under the Clause is not to denigrate it as the Court suggests. Chief Justice [John] Marshall stated of the Confrontation Clause: "I know of no principle in the preservation of which all are more concerned. I know none, by undermining which, life, liberty and property, might be more endangered. It is therefore incumbent on courts to be watchful of every inroad on a principle so truly important." Yet, he recognized that such a right was not absolute, acknowledging that exceptions to the exclusionary component of the hearsay rule, which he considered as an "inroad" on the right to confrontation, had been introduced.

Exceptions to confrontation have always been derived from the experience that some out-of-court statements are just as reliable as cross-examined in-court testimony due to the circumstances under which they were made. We have recognized, for example, that co-conspirator statements simply "cannot be replicated, even if the declarant testifies to the same matters in court." *United States* v. *Inadi*, 475 U. S. 387, 395 (1986). Because the statements are made while the declarant and the accused are partners in an illegal enterprise, the statements are unlikely to be false and their admission "actually furthers the 'Confrontation Clause's very mission' which is to 'advance the accuracy of the truth-determining process in criminal trials.'" Similar reasons justify the introduction of spontaneous declarations, statements made in the course of procuring medical services, dying declarations, and countless other hearsay exceptions. That a statement might be testimonial does nothing to undermine the wisdom of one of these exceptions.

Indeed, cross-examination is a tool used to flesh out the truth, not an empty procedure. . . . "[I]n a given instance [cross-examination may] be superfluous; it may be sufficiently clear, in that instance, that the statement offered is free enough from the risk of inaccuracy and untrustworthiness, so that the test of cross-examination would be a work of supererogation." 5 Wigmore §1420, at 251. In such a case, as we noted over 100 years ago, "The law in its wisdom declares that the rights of the public shall not be wholly sacrificed in order that an incidental benefit may be preserved to the accused." *Mattox* [v. *United States*], 156 U. S., at 243. By creating an immutable category of excluded evidence, the Court adds little to a trial's truth-finding function and ignores this longstanding guidance.

Overruling *Roberts*

In choosing the path it does, the Court of course overrules *Ohio* v. *Roberts*, 448 U. S. 56 (1980), a case decided nearly a quarter of a century ago. *Stare decisis* [the need to follow earlier decisions] is not an inexorable command in the area of constitutional law, but by and large, it "is the preferred course because it promotes the evenhanded, predictable, and consistent development of legal principles, fosters reliance on judicial decisions, and contributes to the actual and perceived integrity of the judicial process." And in making this appraisal, doubt that the new rule is indeed the "right" one should surely be weighed in the balance. Though there are no vested interests involved, unresolved questions for the future of everyday criminal trials throughout the country surely counsel the same sort of caution. The Court grandly declares that "[w]e leave for another day any effort to spell out a comprehensive definition of 'testimonial.'" But the thousands of federal prosecutors and the tens of thousands of state prosecutors need answers as to what beyond the specific kinds of "testimony" the Court lists, is covered by the new rule. They need them now, not months or years from now. Rules of criminal evidence are applied every day in courts throughout the country, and parties should not be left in the dark in this manner.

To its credit, the Court's analysis of "testimony" excludes at least some hearsay exceptions, such as business records and official records. To hold otherwise would require numerous additional witnesses without any apparent gain in the truth-seeking process. Likewise to the Court's credit is its implicit recognition that the mistaken application of its new rule by courts which guess wrong as to the scope of the rule is subject to harmless-error analysis.

But these are palliatives to what I believe is a mistaken change of course. It is a change of course not in the least necessary to reverse the judgment of the Supreme Court of Washington in this case. The result the Court reaches follows inexorably from *Roberts* and its progeny without any need for overruling that line of cases. In *Idaho* v. *Wright*, 497 U. S. 805. 820–824 (1990), we held that an out-of-court statement was not admissible simply because the truthfulness of that statement was corroborated by other evidence at trial. As the Court notes, the Supreme Court of Washington gave decisive weight to the "interlocking nature of the two statements." No re-weighing of the "reliability factors," which is hypothesized by the Court . . . is required to reverse the judgment here. A citation to *Idaho* v. *Wright, supra* [above], would suffice. For the reasons stated, I believe that this would be a far preferable course for the Court to take here.

> "Whether you view the Crawford deci-
> sion as favorable to criminal defendants
> or as a wake up call for our criminal
> justice system ... prosecution of sexual
> assault and domestic violence cases ...
> are impacted by this decision."

Crawford Will Have a Significant Impact on Sexual Assault and Child Abuse Cases

Catherine A. Carroll

This article by Catherine A. Carroll, a staff attorney for the Washington (State) Coalition of Sexual Assault Programs, reviews the Crawford decision and discusses the disproportionate impact of the newly articulated test on particular types of cases. Specifically, she asserts that the greatest impact will be upon sexual assault, child abuse, and domestic abuse cases, in which victims are frequently the only witnesses and later availability to testify in court can be lost either through a finding of incompetence (for example, because of a child's age) or by the victim's own desire not to prosecute a loved one. Carroll provides a straightforward review of how the Supreme Court decision will be applied to this very sensitive group of criminal prosecutions and predicts a wide-reaching dampening effect on convictions.

C rawford v. Washington is an important U.S. Supreme Court decision because it impacts the way prosecutors may get evidence; e.g. testimonial statements, admitted into

Catherine A. Carroll, "Understanding *Crawford v. Washington*," *Washington Coalition of Sexual Assault Programs*, October 7, 2004. Reproduced by permission.

court to assist in the prosecution of criminal defendants. *Crawford* involved a criminal defendant's constitutional right to confront his accusers. Specifically the U.S. Supreme Court addressed the issue of whether a criminal defendant's Sixth Amendment Right, under the U.S. Constitution, to confront his or her accusers, known as the "confrontation clause," was violated when the defendant was not afforded an opportunity to cross-examine the "accuser." The Sixth Amendment guarantees that "[i]n all criminal prosecutions, the accused shall enjoy the right . . . to be confronted with the witnesses against him."

Prior to the *Crawford* decision, hearsay[1] statements could withstand a confrontation clause challenge if the statement bore adequate "indicia of reliability," or "particularized guarantees of trustworthiness." In short, prior to *Crawford*, if a victim/witness in a criminal proceeding was not available to testify in court and the defense *did not* have a prior opportunity to cross-examine the victim/witness, their testimonial statements could and often would be admissible in court under a specific, firmly rooted exception to the hearsay rule, such as statements for the purpose of medical diagnosis and [so-called] excited utterances.

The Impact on Sexual Assault Criminal Cases

Generally, *Crawford* only impacts criminal cases when a victim/witness of sexual assault makes testimonial statements and then later is not available to testify in court about those testimonial statements. What constitutes a testimonial statement—given the range of statements a victim of sexual assault may make, how it is made, and to whom, is much of where the impact of *Crawford* is focused.

---

1. *Hearsay* is a statement, other than one made by the declarant while testifying at the trial or hearing, offered as evidence to prove the truth of the matter asserted. Hearsay evidence is testimony in court of a statement made outside of court, the statement being offered as an assertion to show the truth of matters asserted therein, and thus resting for its value upon the credibility of the out-of-court asserter.

Although the Court declined to fully articulate what exactly constitutes a testimonial statement, they did refer to extrajudicial statements . . . contained in formalized testimonial materials, such as affidavits, depositions, prior testimony or confessions, as testimonial. Further the Court said that testimonial statements include those "made under circumstances which would lead an objective witness reasonably to believe that the statement would be available for use at a later trial."

The Impact on Child and Domestic Abuse Cases

Therefore it is likely that a statement made by a victim/witness of sexual assault to a police officer, child protective services or adult protective services agent, will be considered testimonial. Furthermore, the impact may vary depending on the victim's age. For example, child victims of sexual assault who are not available to testify in court because they are too young and have been found incompetent may be more adversely impacted by the *Crawford* decision. This is because *Crawford* is about allowing the accused the opportunity to confront their accusers. Thus if the child victim is unavailable to testify and defense counsel did not have an opportunity to question the child, and the statements are not admissible under a firmly rooted exception to the hearsay rule, it may be that the child's statements regarding the sexual abuse will not be admissible.

Similarly in domestic violence criminal cases where a victim of domestic violence refuses to testify against her batterer, and defense counsel did not have an opportunity to cross-examine the victim, it is unlikely her statements made out of court about the domestic violence incident will be admissible against the defendant/batterer. Because it is not uncommon for a victim of sexual assault or domestic violence to be the only witness to the assault, it is more difficult to prosecute these cases if the victims are not available to testify and if defense counsel did not have an opportunity to cross-examine them. This is why some people have suggested that evidence-based prosecution in domestic violence cases may no longer be a viable strategy.

The impact of *Crawford* on sexual assault victims, adult and children, will continue to unfold as this case is applied to various fact patterns all over the country. Whether you view the *Crawford* decision as favorable to criminal defendants or as a wake up call for our criminal justice system, across the country, every state's prosecution of sexual assault and domestic violence cases, to varying degrees of significance, are impacted by this decision.

In summary, *Crawford* applies only when *all* the following elements occur:

- Criminal prosecution

- The case involves "testimonial" evidence made by the victim/witness

- The victim is unavailable to testify in court, and

- The defendant did not have a prior opportunity to cross-examine the victim/witness.

> *"[The* Crawford *decision] has, in es-
> sence, radically shifted the balance of
> power from prosecutors to reluctant
> complainants."*

Crawford Makes Prosecution of Domestic Violence More Difficult

David Feige

*The prosecution of domestic violence cases has long been compli-
cated by the potential infliction of psychological suffering on the
victims in court aside from their physical abuse by violence.
Whether driven by love for their batterers, unhealthy psychological dependence, or embarrassment connected with airing personal troubles, the reality of the situation is that it is common
for victims to not want to prosecute. In this article, New York
public defender David Feige describes a real-world result of the
Crawford v. Washington decision: Prosecution of domestic abusers without the cooperation of the victims and based on outside
evidence such as 911 calls, filed complaints, or domestic violence
reports signed the day after the assault, is now much more difficult. Ironically termed "evidence-based" prosecution, the entry of
this kind of evidence without in-court testimony by the victim,
Feige argues, has effectively been eliminated by the Crawford
holding.*

On the third floor of the drab concrete box that is the
Bronx Criminal Court, Judges Ruth Levine Sussman and
Diane Kiesel preside over courtrooms filled with domestic

David Feige, "Domestic Silence: The Supreme Court Kills Evidence-Based Prosecution," *Slate*, March 12, 2004. Copyright © 2004 United Feature Syndicate, Inc. All
rights reserved. Reproduced by permission of the author.

violence cases—often 75 in a single day. Like many veteran public defenders, I hate domestic violence cases. They are highly charged, emotionally complicated, and very hard to defend. They're hard to defend because these courts dispense a rather specialized kind of justice. In these cases, specially trained prosecutors plead cases before judges who've been specially trained to be "especially sensitive" to a particular kind of crime. What that means in practice is that many judges like Kiesel and Sussman who hear domestic violence cases have attended seminars that make them ideologically sympathetic to the prosecution. Part of that "special training" and "special sensitivity" seems to be accepting the notion that prosecutors—rather than the alleged victims themselves—know what is best for those alleged victims. Defending a domestic violence case against a prosecutor who claims to speak for the victim, in front of a judge who is generally sympathetic to the prosecution, can be bad for a criminal defendant and pretty much ruin a public defender's day. Mercifully, the U.S. Supreme Court, in the unlikely personage of Justice Antonin Scalia, just made life in the domestic violence courts a lot more pleasant for both defendants and public defenders.

The Reluctant Complainant

One of the peculiar realities of domestic violence cases is that—abused or not—the complaining witnesses often don't want their loved ones prosecuted. Thanks to the Supreme Court, many more of those victims are about to get their wish. [The] decision in *Crawford v. Washington*, which reversed the assault conviction of Michael Crawford—sentenced to 14 1/2 years in prison for stabbing a man he believed had tried to rape his wife—was overtly about the Constitution's confrontation clause. But the ruling will radically change the prosecution of domestic violence cases throughout the country, empowering complainants to resist the demands of prosecutors and limiting the number of cases that proceed with unwilling witnesses.

It is not uncommon for alleged victims and prosecutors to have divergent agendas. This divergence can become particularly acute when prosecutors proceed with a case despite an alleged victim's desires. Prosecutors are, of course, within their rights to do this—there is no question that once an arrest is made, it is up to the state to prosecute or not, regardless of a victim's wishes—that's why criminal actions are captioned the *People v. Someone* or the *United States of America v. Someone Else*. But while pursuing a prosecution despite the express wishes of the alleged victim is rare in the average case, in domestic violence cases it's commonplace.

Domestic cases are emotionally complex—far more so than most criminal cases. In the last decade or so, mandatory arrest policies—designed to eliminate police discretion in domestic incidents—have dragged into the system a large number of cases that might, in an earlier age, have died on the doorstep. As a result, the system is deluged with cases in which the supposed victims either don't consider themselves victims or want nothing to do with the prosecution of their alleged abusers. Even in cases alleging serious abuse, the nuances of the intimate relationship between the parties and the brutality of the system often make complainants who start out cooperative ultimately wish the whole case would just go away. As a consequence, domestic violence cases, more often than any others, go to trial with unwilling or unavailable witnesses. Almost every day in courts around the country, prosecutors reach into their bag of tricks in an attempt to wheedle, cajole, or intimidate reluctant complainants in such cases into testifying against their current or former intimate partners.

Forcing the Witness

And when wheedling, cajoling, or intimidation doesn't work, prosecutors are left with a difficult choice: They can try to force a complainant to testify by securing what is known as a material witness order—essentially an arrest warrant—or they can try to proceed without the witness. Though not unheard of, dragging the alleged victim into court in handcuffs and forcing her to testify is generally considered unseemly. It is also often counterproductive, since a witness hellbent on avoiding testifying will rarely provide the kind of performance prosecutors can rely on for a conviction.

Because of the reluctance to force resistant complainants to testify, in case after case, in courtrooms around the country, prosecutors have been left to try to prove their cases using a paper trail—a call to 911, a criminal complaint signed the day after the charges, or a domestic incident report signed the night of the arrest. Judges, especially those trained to be "especially sensitive" to the issues in domestic violence cases, almost invariably find these papers reliable and admit them into evidence, facilitating an entire prosecution in which the defendant never gets to ask the accuser a single question. This is what's termed, in a rather Orwellian turn of phrase [i.e., in government "doublespeak"], an "evidence-based prosecution," and it is precisely this sort of prosecution that the Supreme Court has just shut down with the 9-0 decision in *Crawford*.

The *Crawford* Decision

In a dense opinion studded with historical references, Justice [Antonin] Scalia held that the Sixth Amendment's guarantee of the right of an accused to "be confronted with the witnesses against him" meant just that—that prosecutors who want to use testimonial statements made by unavailable witnesses who haven't yet been subjected to cross-examination, quite simply, can't.

For nearly a quarter century, prosecutors have capitalized on the old rule—articulated 24 years ago in *Ohio v. Roberts*—that a statement from an unavailable witness can still be used if a judge found other indicia of reliability. This left the majority of the case in the judge's hands. As Scalia put it, "Admitting statements deemed reliable by a judge is fundamentally at odds with the right of confrontation. Dispensing with confrontation because testimony is obviously reliable is akin to dispensing with jury trial because a defendant is obviously guilty. This is not what the Sixth Amendment prescribes."

Indeed, in one of the most acerbic sections of the decision, Scalia dismisses the *Roberts* rule, calling it "amorphous," "subjective," and "unpredictable." As he notes, "Some courts wind up attaching the same significance to opposite facts. For example the Colorado Supreme Court held a statement more reliable because its inculpation of the defendant was 'detailed' ... while the Fourth Circuit found a statement more reliable because the portion implicating another was 'fleeting.'" The problem with such vague standards, as Scalia candidly observes, is that they are "manipulable."

What Scalia was too polite to say, but what most veteran criminal lawyers already know—and what most first-year law students learn—is that in the criminal justice system, such flexible, subjective "standards" regularly devolve into purely political decisions. In the context of domestic violence court, that means that judges such as Kiesel and Sussman will regularly admit the calls, complaints, and incident reports, preferring to find indicia of reliability rather than force a prosecutor into the Hobson's choice of a material witness order or a dismissal.

The *Crawford* decision, by insisting on the right of an accused to confront the witness, rather than just a tape recording or police report, wipes away a judge's ability to admit any of this evidence without the actual witness being subject to cross-examination. As a consequence, prosecutors unwilling to arrest and jail their own witnesses on material witness orders have lost one of the most powerful weapons in their arsenal— the fact that, at least until *Crawford*, they often didn't need a victim's testimony to make a case.

Bright-Line Rule for Big-Ticket Cases

Crawford was never styled as a populist opinion. On the contrary, Scalia seems to profess a certain disdain for what he describes as "run of the mill assault cases," explaining that the clear rule he annunciates is mostly necessary to insulate the accused in the great state trials involving politically charged issues—those of, say, Sir Walter Raleigh [tried for treason in seventeenth-century England] or Jose Padilla [arrested as a terrorist in 2002]. But as he fashions a new bright-line rule for the big-ticket cases, Scalia either ignores or forgets the sad daily truth of local domestic violence courtrooms: that ideologically driven judicial decision-making is alive and well even in run of the mill assault cases.

Whether he knew it or not, Scalia has, in essence, radically shifted the balance of power from prosecutors to reluctant complainants, giving alleged victims more control over the cases of their own victimization and greater freedom from the paternalistic philosophy of prosecution that the *Roberts* rule enabled. So from now on, when the complainant in a domestic violence case insists she's not coming to court and just wants to drop the charges, I'll just smile as Judge Kiesel says, "Case dismissed."

"The time is ripe for the Court to satisfy its promise to fill in the blanks it intentionally left when it decided Crawford v. Washington.*"*

The Supreme Court Continues to Interpret the Confrontation Clause After *Crawford*

Leonard Post

When the Supreme Court decided Crawford v. Washington, *it opened the door to new challenges involving the application of the new test for admissibility of evidence from unavailable witnesses set forth in that decision. One of the most important of these questions was the dividing line between testimonial and nontestimonial statements. This division is important, as the Supreme Court was clear in* Crawford *that the new absolute requirement that a witness appear and be available for cross-examination would apply only to testimony. Thus, lower courts have struggled to categorize various kinds of statements—excited utterances made during 911 calls and during interviews with police responding to reports of domestic disturbances, for example—as testimony or nontestimony. To try to provide more guidance, the Court in 2006 reviewed two cases together that involved such scenarios. The following article by legal analyst Leonard Post describes the three camps that lower courts have fallen into when dealing with the issue of confronting one's accusers.*

Leonard Post, "All Eyes Are on High Court over '*Crawford*' Issues," *National Law Journal*, October 27, 2005. Copyright © 2005, ALM Properties, Inc. Republished with permission of National Law Journal, conveyed through Copyright Clearance Center, Inc.

The outcomes of thousands of criminal cases hang in the balance while the U.S. Supreme Court decides whether to clarify when out-of-court accusations may be used in lieu of in-court testimony without violating defendants' Sixth Amendment right to confront witnesses.

Both the National District Attorneys Association's [NDAA] point man on the confrontation clause and the National Association of Criminal Defense Lawyers [NACDL] agree that the time is ripe for the Court to satisfy its promise to fill in the blanks it intentionally left when it decided *Crawford v. Washington*, 541 U.S. 36 (2004).

Two petitions for certiorari [Supreme Court review] that raise confrontation clause issues—in the context of excited utterance exceptions to hearsay rules—are pending before the court. Both *Davis v. Washington*, No. 05-5224, and *Hammon v. Indiana*, No. 05-5705, domestic violence cases, are listed for action by the court at its Oct. 28 [2005] conference. The court's decision on whether it will hear the cases is expected on Oct. 31.[1]

Before *Crawford*, any hearsay could come in—even when a witness did not testify—if the hearsay exception was firmly rooted and traditional, and if a judge found the statement to be reliable and trustworthy in the circumstances in which it was made. *Ohio v. Roberts*, 448 U.S. 56 (1989).

Crawford bars testimonial hearsay introduced by the prosecution unless the defense has an opportunity to question the person who made the statement and that person is unavailable at the time of trial. With some exceptions, the court explicitly decided that it would "leave for another day" a more specific definition of "testimonial."

While domestic violence prosecutions make up the bulk of these kinds of cases, the issues also have arisen in murder,

---

1. The U.S. Supreme Court decided to hear both of these cases as "companion cases" on this day. Arguments were heard March 23, 2006. In June 2006 the Court decided that frantic emergency 911 utterances were *not* testimonial (*Davis*) but post-emergency interview statements as part of a criminal investigation *were* testimonial (*Hammon*).

robbery, burglary, assault and other criminal matters. "The pro-defense, anti-government crowd is interpreting *Crawford* with shocking overbreadth," said Richard Wintory, a Pima County, Ariz., deputy county attorney and an NDAA board member. "On the other side, you see some prosecutors acting as if the Supreme Court didn't mean what it was saying."

Barbara Bergman, president of the NACDL and a visiting professor at Washington [D.C.]'s Catholic University of America Columbus School of Law, noted the "tremendous confusion in federal and state court decisions as to the meaning of 'testimonial' in the context of *Crawford*.

"Judges have struggled to see where particular cases fit—like 911 calls—that fall between the cracks of the concrete definitions of testimonial that the court laid out," Bergman said. . . .

Three Camps

Since the high court decided *Crawford*, federal circuit, state supreme and intermediate appellate courts have divided into three camps. Each camp uses a different rationale in determining when, and if, tapes of 911 calls and statements taken by investigating police officers at alleged crime scenes are testimonial.

A few courts have found that 911 calls and witness statements made to police investigators who come to scenes of recent alleged crimes are nontestimonial. Therefore, they find *Crawford* inapplicable, and those alleged witnesses are not required to testify.

On the other end of the spectrum, many courts find that all statements that come after an alleged crime has been completed are testimonial, and therefore the person who made the statement must be available for cross-examination.

More courts say that whether or not a statement is testimonial depends on the circumstances, but there is wide disparity among those courts as to what those circumstances are.

Some courts say that it depends on a speaker's purpose in making a statement and a government agent's actions at the time. Some say it depends on whether the statements were generated to bear witness or were attempts to be rescued from peril. Some say the test for that is subjective; others say it is objective. Some say only those statements made before alleged crime scenes are secured are not testimonial. Some courts focus on the formality or informality of the communication, or whether an adversarial relationship existed between those making the statements and the police. Who initiated the conversation is important to some courts, as is the motivation of the interviewers.

The *Davis* Case

Michelle McCottry called 911 in February 2001, and said that someone had just beaten her up. For about four minutes, responding to questions, McCottry described the alleged crime and identified Adrian Davis, who had allegedly left the scene before the call. When police arrived, they noted fresh injuries on her forearm and face.

At trial, McCottry was not called to testify. The 911 tape was played and the prosecutor told the jury that though she hadn't testified, she "had left you something better. She left you her testimony on the day that this happened." It was the only evidence introduced that Davis and not someone else had beaten her up.

In an 8-1 ruling, the Washington Supreme Court decided that McCottry's statement was not testimonial. *State v. Davis*, 111 P.3d 844. The majority's reasoning was that she had called 911 because she was in immediate danger, not to assist police in an investigation.

"This is a false dichotomy," asserted Jeffrey Fisher, a partner with Seattle's Davis Wright Tremaine [law firm].

"When a person requests police assistance, their accusations must be treated as testimonial because people also realize that such reports are likely to trigger criminal investigations or prosecutions," he said.

"Otherwise, anytime a person called 911—or the police or the DA [district attorney]—and reported a crime, the caller's statements would not be testimonial. This is impossible to reconcile with having a right to confront one's accuser," said Fisher, who argued *Crawford* before the U.S. Supreme Court.

Washington prosecutors disagree.

"A fundamental problem with the allegedly 'objective' standard [that] petitioner urges on the court is that no statement beyond a bare initial plea for help—perhaps just a shriek into the telephone receiver—can come in. The remainder of the call would be excluded," said James Whisman, King County [Washington] senior deputy prosecuting attorney.

"I do not believe the framers [of the Constitution] intended the confrontation clause to bar such evidence. They also assert that every 911 operator is conducting an interrogation, which is certainly not the case," he said.

The *Hammon* Case

Responding to a domestic violence call at the house of Hershel Hammon and his wife, Amy, police found evidence of an altercation. Amy denied there had been a problem. Hershel, in another room, told police there had been an argument, but that things were now fine.

When questioned again, Amy said that he had punched her twice in the chest and thrown her to the ground onto broken glass. She then filled out a form affidavit, which laid out statutory battery allegations, and wrote a specific description of what Hershel had allegedly done. The form said that the investigating officer would rely on her statements to establish probable cause for an arrest.

At the bench trial, Amy, who had been subpoenaed to testify, didn't show up. The judge admitted officers' testimony of Amy's oral statements as an excited utterance and her affidavit as a present-sense exception to the hearsay rules. Hershel was convicted. The Indiana Supreme Court found that the motivation of a government agent questioning a witness was more determinative—for the purpose of future legal use of a statement—than the motivation of the witness, but if either were motivated by a desire to preserve the statement, it would be sufficient to render the statement testimonial.

"[R]esponses to initial inquiries by officers arriving at a scene are typically not testimonial," the court said. *Hammon v. State*, 829 N.E.2d 444 (2005). The other aspect the court addressed was that the officers were there to secure and assess the scene, not for the purpose of gathering evidence for use at trial.

Richard Friedman, Hershel Hammon's lead counsel before the U.S. Supreme Court and a professor at the University of Michigan Law School, said that the court got it wrong.

"The decisive criterion is not a witness's—in this case the accuser's—subjective purpose or motivation, but rather whether a reasonable person in her position would anticipate that the statement would likely be used in investigating or prosecuting a crime," said Friedman.

It depends on the circumstances, said Indiana Solicitor General Thomas M. Fisher, the prosecution's counsel of record in *Hammon*. "Particularly in domestic violence situations it is important that police have the leeway to carefully assess the scene before victim statements are deemed testimonial," Fisher said. "The confrontation clause should not be construed in a way that would discourage police from determining whether the victim needs immediate protection."

Organizations to Contact

The editors have compiled the following list of organizations concerned with the issues debated in this book. The descriptions are derived from materials provided by the organizations. All have publications or information available for interested readers. The list was compiled on the date of publication of the present volume; names, addresses, and phone numbers may change. Be aware that many organizations take several weeks or longer to respond to inquiries, so allow as much time as possible.

American Bar Association (ABA)
321 N. Clark St., Chicago, IL 60610
(312) 988-5000
e-mail: askaba@abanet.org
Web site: www.abanet.org

The American Bar Association is the largest voluntary professional association in the world. With more than four hundred thousand members, the ABA provides law school accreditation, continuing legal education, information about the law, programs to assist lawyers and judges in their work, and initiatives to improve the legal system for the public. Its comprehensive Web site maintains archives of documents and articles concerning the right to counsel, the right to a jury trial, and the confrontation clause.

American Civil Liberties Union (ACLU)
125 Broad St., 18th Fl., New York, NY 10004
(212) 549-2500 • fax: (212) 549-2646
Web site: www.aclu.org

The ACLU is a nonprofit and nonpartisan organization that works to protect individual rights guaranteed under the Constitution through court cases, legislative lobbying, and public information initiatives. The ACLU Web site includes numerous press releases and reports documenting the organization's efforts to provide counsel to indigent defendants, upholding the right to a jury trial, and the role of the presumption of innocence in the current political climate.

Cato Institute

1000 Massachusetts Ave. NW, Washington, DC   20001
(202) 842-0200 • fax: (202) 842-3490
e-mail: cato@cato.org
Web site: www.cato.org

The Cato Institute is a libertarian think tank that asserts traditional American principles of limited government, individual liberty, free markets and peace. The institute advocates public policy based on these principles and the involvement of an intelligent, concerned lay public in questions of policy and the proper role of government. Numerous articles addressing the rights of the accused, published originally in the institute's magazine *Regulation* or in periodic policy reports, are available on its Web site.

Center for Constitutional Rights (CCR)

666 Broadway, 7th Fl., New York, NY   10012
(212) 614-6464 • fax: (212) 614-6499
e-mail: info@ccr-ny.org
Web site: www.ccr-ny.org

CCR is a nonprofit organization that supports legal action and education to protect and advance the rights guaranteed by the U.S. Constitution and the Universal Declaration of Human Rights. Reports available on its Web site address the right to counsel and the right to a jury trial, particularly in the context of prisoners being detained at Guantánamo, Cuba.

Criminal Justice Legal Foundation (CJLF)

PO Box 1199, Sacramento, CA   95812
(916) 446-0345
e-mail: cjlf@cjlf.org
Web site: www.cjlf.org

CJLF is a public interest organization that works to protect and support the rights of crime victims. Although focused on support of the death penalty, CJLF has been involved in court cases involving rights of the accused, including the right to a jury trial and the right to counsel. Its Web site includes a publication addressing the right to counsel for children who are victims of crime and hosts a blog called "Crime and Consequences" (www.crimeandconsequences.com).

National Association of Criminal Defense Lawyers (NACDL)
1150 Eighteenth St. NW, Ste. 950, Washington, DC   20006
(202) 872-8600 • fax: (202) 872-8690
e-mail: assist@nacdl.org
Web site: www.nacdl.org

NACDL is a bar association that works to ensure justice and due process for persons accused of crime or other misconduct. The organization is particularly active in providing counsel to indigent defendants. NACDL publishes *Champions* magazine and several articles about the confrontation right and the right to counsel are available on its Web site.

National Legal Aid & Defender Association (NLADA)
1140 Connecticut Ave. NW, Ste. 900, Washington, DC   20036
(202) 452-0620 • fax: (202) 872-1031
Web site: www.nlada.org

NLADA provides educational products and services advocating equal justice for all and acts as a national voice in public policy and legislative debates. NLADA also serves as a resource for those seeking more information on equal justice in the United States. Its Web site includes a searchable e-library that includes numerous reports, articles, and other publications about the rights of the accused.

For Further Research

Books

Ronald Banaszak, ed., *Fair Trial Rights of the Accused: A Documentary History*. Westport, CT: Greenwood, 2002.

Walter M. Brasch, *America's Unpatriotic Acts: The Federal Government's Violation of Constitutional and Civil Rights*. New York: Peter Lang, 2005.

Andrea S. Campbell, *The Rights of the Accused*. New York: Chelsea House, 2001.

William L. Dwyer, *In the Hands of the People: The Trial Jury's Origins, Triumphs, Troubles, and Future in American Democracy*. New York: St Martin's Griffin, 2004.

Adam Fairclough, *Race and Democracy: The Civil Rights Struggle in Louisiana, 1915–1972*. Athens: University of Georgia Press, 1999.

Kermit L. Hall, *The Rights of the Accused: The Justices and Criminal Justice*. New York: Garland, 2000.

Anthony Lewis, *Gideon's Trumpet*. New York: Random House, 1964.

John J. Patrick, *The Supreme Court of the United States: A Student Companion*. New York: Oxford University Press, 2002.

John J. Patrick, Richard M. Pious, and Donald A. Ritchie, *Oxford Guide to the United States Government*. New York: Oxford University Press, 2001.

Fred Ramen, *The Rights of the Accused: Individual Rights and Civic Responsibility*. New York: Rosen, 2001.

William H. Rehnquist, *The Supreme Court*. New York: Vintage, 2002.

Melvin I. Urofsky, *The Continuity of Change: The Supreme Court and Individual Liberties, 1953–1986*. Belmont, CA: Wadsworth, 1989.

Robert Winters, ed., *The Bill of Rights: The Right to a Trial by Jury*. San Diego: Greenhaven, 2005.

Periodicals

General

Mona Eltahawy, "Preserving Rights in a Terrorized World," *Washington Post*, June 1, 2003.

Coffin v. United States

Richard Friedman, "A Presumption of Innocence, Not of Even Odds," *Stanford Law Review*, vol. 52, April 1, 2000.

Isabel Gibson, "From Richard III to Michael: A Presumption of Innocence," *Bergen County* (NJ) *Record*, February 7, 2005.

Bruce Schneier, "Guilty Until Proven Innocent?" *IEEE Security & Privacy*, vol. 1, no. 3, May/June 2003.

Alexander Volokh, "On Guilty Men," *University of Pennsylvania Law Review*, vol. 146, no. 173, 1997.

Gideon v. Wainwright

Stephen B. Bright, "*Gideon*'s Reality: After Four Decades, Where Are We?" *Criminal Justice*, vol. 18, no. 2, summer 2003.

Edward M. Kennedy, "What 'Gideon' Promised," *Legal Times*, March 28, 2003.

Douglas McCollam, "The Ghost of 'Gideon,'" *American Lawyer*, March 4, 2003.

Bill Rankin, "Right to Lawyer Still Not a Given for Poor Defendants," *Atlanta Journal-Constitution*, March 24, 2003.

Duncan v. Louisiana

Barbara Bradley, "Juries and Justice: Is the System Obsolete?" *Insight on the News*, April 24, 1995.

Jeff E. Butler, "Petty Offenses, Serious Consequences: Multiple Petty Offenses and the Right to Jury Trial," *Michigan Law Review*, vol. 93, 1995.

Patty Dineen, "Reaching a Verdict: What Do We Want for the American Jury System?" report from the American Bar Association, 2005.

Timothy Lynch, "The Case Against Plea Bargaining: Government Should Not Retaliate Against Individuals Who Exercise Their Right to Trial by Jury," *Regulation*, vol. 26, no. 3, fall 2003.

Crawford v. Washington

Robert W. Best, "To Be or Not to Be Testimonial? That Is the Question: 2004 Developments in the Sixth Amendment," *Army Lawyer*, April 2005.

Richard D. Friedman, "The Confrontation Clause Re-rooted and Transformed," *Cato Supreme Court Review*, 2004–2005.

Laird Kirkpatrick, "*Crawford*: A Look Backward, a Look Forward," *Criminal Justice*, vol. 20, no. 2, Summer 2005.

Miguel A. Mendez, "*Crawford v. Washington*: A Critique," *Stanford Law Review*, November 1, 2004.

Daniel E. Monnat, "The Kid Gloves Are Off: Child Hearsay After *Crawford v. Washington*," National Association of Criminal Lawyers (NACDL) News, January/February 2006.

Ariana J. Torchin, "A Multidimensional Framework for the Analysis of Testimonial Hearsay Under *Crawford v. Washington*," *Georgetown Law Journal*, vol. 94, issue 2, 2006.

John F. Yetter, "Wrestling with *Crawford v. Washington* and the New Constitutional Law of Confrontation," *Florida Bar Journal*, October 1, 2004.

Internet Sources

General

U.S. Department of State, "Rights of the Accused," *Rights of the People*, December 2003. http://usinfo.state.gov/products/pubs/rightsof/accused.htm.

Coffin v. United States

Erin Murphy, "The Presumption of Sexual Guilt," Center for Individual Freedom, March 4, 2004. www.cfif.org/htdocs/freedomline/current/guest_commentary/presumption_sexual_guilt.htm.

Gideon v. Wainwright

American Bar Association, "*Gideon*'s Broken Promise: American's Continuing Quest for Equal Justice," February 11, 2004. www.abanet.org/legalservices/sclaid/defender/brokenpromise.

National Association of Criminal Defense Lawyers, "*Gideon* at 40: Fulfilling the Promise," March 18, 2003. www.nacdl.org/gideon.

Index